P9-CCF-259

US Economic Development Policies towards the
Pacific Rim

Also by Nan Wiegersma

THE WOMEN, GENDER AND DEVELOPMENT READER (*editor with Nalini Visvamathan, Laurie Nisonoff and Lynn Duggan*)

VIETNAM: Peasant Land, Peasant Revolution

US Economic Development Policies towards the Pacific Rim

Successes and Failures of US Aid

Nan Wiegersma
Professor of Economics
Fitchburg State College

and

Joseph E. Medley
Associate Professor of Economics
University of Southern Maine
Portland

First published in Great Britain 2000 by
MACMILLAN PRESS LTD
Houndmills, Basingstoke, Hampshire RG21 6XS and London
Companies and representatives throughout the world

A catalogue record for this book is available from the British Library.

ISBN 0–333–67014–0 hardcover
ISBN 0–333–80451–1 paperback

First published in the United States of America 2000 by
ST. MARTIN'S PRESS, INC.,
Scholarly and Reference Division,
175 Fifth Avenue, New York, N.Y. 10010

ISBN 0–312–23129–6
ISBN 0–312–23130–X

HC
681
.W54
2000

Library of Congress Cataloging-in-Publication Data
Wiegersma, Nancy.
US economic development policies towards the Pacific rim : successes and
failures of US aid / Nan Wiegersma and Joseph E. Medley.
p.   cm.
Includes bibliographical references and index.
ISBN 0–312–23129–6 (cloth) — ISBN 0–312–23130–X (pbk.)
1. Pacific Area—Economic conditions. 2. Asia—Economic conditions. 3.
Economic assistance, American—Pacific Area. 4. Economic assistance,
American—Asia. I. Medley, Joseph E. II. Title.

HC681 .W54   2000
338.91'7301823—dc21   99–054920

This book is printed on paper suitable for recycling and made from fully managed and sustained
forest sources.

10   9   8   7   6   5   4   3   2   1
09   08   07   06   05   04   03   02   01   00

Printed and bound in Great Britain by
Antony Rowe Ltd, Chippenham, Wiltshire

To our children

Nan's daughter, *Chandra Hancock*
Joe's sons, *Patrik Medley* and *Niklas Caner-Medley*

Contents

List of Tables and Figures

Preface

The financial crisis that engulfed many Asian countries in 1997–8 has allowed the US and important international economic agencies to question the continued efficacy of the East Asian model of development. In particular, the crisis has served as an occasion for the International Monetary Fund (IMF) to provide over $100 billion of emergency aid to the affected Asian economies under the condition that they restructure their economies according to IMF 'structural adjustment programs.' These reform programs require trade liberalization; open and deregulated financial markets; and 'Western' accounting, financial, and legal practices that favor established banks and corporations from developed countries. Through the structural adjustment programs, the IMF acts as a global central bank that regulates the financial systems and economic policies of the international capitalist economy according to the development ideology promoted by the US and its closest allies. The Asian countries, including Japan, are resisting many of these reforms because, if fully implemented, they will dismantle what has up to now been a successful model of economic development.

The IMF, rather than the US government, has controlled the flow of most US aid to Pacific Rim countries during the Asian financial crisis. The general perception that the key international financial agencies, in particular the IMF and the World Bank, are controlled by and benefit the international community is wrong. IMF policy represents a 'Washington Consensus' – forged primarily by the US – that good economic development performance requires macroeconomic stability, with the stress on low rates of inflation, and increasing reliance on markets through trade and financial deregulation and privatization. In other words, the IMF is the lead agency in an effort directed by the US to reduce Asian governmental intervention. Without government intervention, private firms can, it is alleged, more efficiently guide economic activity along the path to increased growth and improved welfare. Our interpretation, however, is that the East Asian growth-with-equity model is under serious attack because the Asian economies are now vulnerable to financial pressure. Their current vulnerability has made it possible for global capitalists, represented by the IMF, to push for the elimination of Asian financial and trade regulations that are costly to their firms.

Opposition to IMF policies is brewing among some Clinton administration and World Bank officials. For example, Joseph Stiglitz, former chair of the President's Council of Economic Advisors and currently Chief Economist at the World Bank, has added his voice (Stiglitz 1998a) to those who question the merits and point out the limits of the 'laissez-faire' aid policies forged during the Reagan–Bush era. Along with some of his World Bank colleagues and liberal members of the Clinton administration, he argues that development also requires government intervention to ensure sound financial regulation, effective competition policy, transfer of technology, and access to international markets as well as to institute policies that support sustainable, egalitarian and democratic development. In our book, we show that several East Asian countries developed a model that achieved exactly those goals with US aid in the 1950s and 1960s. We also show that the US subsequently departed from those successful approaches and, in Vietnam and parts of Central America, began to formulate the model that serves as the foundation for the IMF's current policy interventions.

In the late 1980s and early 1990s the Japanese challenged the structural adjustment inequities enforced by the IMF in the interests of the 'Washington Consensus.' It is ironic that, at a moment when the East Asian economies, including Japan's, are facing difficulties, the IMF is extending its efforts to dismantle the East Asian development model. How is the East Asian financial crisis connected to recent deregulatory pressures imposed on East Asian countries by the US? Have consequent East Asian 'reforms' contributed to the crises these countries face in the late 1990s? Our first chapter describes the IMF/World Bank structural adjustment model and then contrasts it to the East Asian model. The following chapters outline case studies that exemplify the effects of each approach. Our conclusion elucidates the recent effects of increased globalization in the various countries, the genesis and unfolding of East Asia's financial crisis, and some lessons concerning economic development and US interventions in an increasingly global economy.

NAN WIEGERSMA
JOSEPH E. MEDLEY

Acknowledgements

We would like to acknowledge the many people who, as individuals and in groups, have contributed to our work on aid and development which has resulted in this book. The New England Women and Development Group critiqued early drafts of Chapter 2, and the Korean sections of Chapter 3 and Chapter 6. The theoretical and historical development of Chapters 1 and 2 was aided by feedback from Laurie Nisonoff, Carmen Diana Deere and James Boyce and from reactions from Nan Wiegersma's September 1990 presentation to the Economic Development and History Seminar at the University of Massachusetts. Stephen Resnick, David Ruccio, Rick Wolff and others from the Association for Economic and Social Analysis helped us form our overview of development theory in Chapter 1. Conversations with John McKeon, Fitchburg State College, were helpful in developing our analysis on the effectiveness of aid in promoting development. Conversations with Jega Arulpragasam helped in the development of the concept of trade advantages.

Chapters 3 and 4 benefitted from the comments and suggestions made by Paul Zarembka and others at the journal *Research in Political Economy*, in which some of this material first appeared. Anthony D'Costa's complementary research efforts, comments and encouragement improved Chapter 4. Ed and Gloria Medley's help with material concerning the 1960s in Taiwan is deeply appreciated. We especially want to thank Ed Medley for sharing the keen insights he gained during his many years spent directing aid programs in East and South Asia.

The work of Nola Reinhardt, Carmen Diana Deere and James Boyce influenced our perspectives on land reform programs in Central America and aid to Central America. Nan Wiegersma's work in 1986–8 with Nola Reinhardt on interviews for a project concerning land reform in Central America was helpful in developing our perspective concerning the impact of aid in that region. Wiegersma's work at Instituto Centroamericano de Administracion Empreses, INCAE, on a Fulbright fellowship in 1991, helped to further develop our perspective. A return visit and research in 1993 was sponsored by Fitchburg State College. We wish to thank the Fulbright Program and Fitchburg State College for their grants.

We also wish to thank the many faculty and staff members at the University of Southern Maine who have assisted our efforts. In particular, the observations and comments freely offered by Michael Hillard to Joseph Medley throughout the writing of this book were invaluable. Professor Hillard has always been an exemplary colleague and a true friend. Professor Lorrayne Carroll read and made helpful comments on each of the book's chapters; however, her firm grasp of both abstract theoretical and practical political issues was most useful in the crafting of Chapter 8.

Help with statistical calculations from a colleague, Pirudas Lwamugira, at Fitchburg State College and a student assistant, Rachellé Lappinen, is acknowledged. John Delvaille greatly helped with the presentation of graphs and tables.

In 1991 and 1993, Nan Wiegersma used the resources of the Ben Linder Center in Managua as well as the Managua section of the Coordinadora Regional de Investigacion Economicas y Sociales (CRIES) and we would like to thank the staffs of these organizations for all their help. Special thanks go to Angel Saldomando of CRIES for sharing his perspectives concerning aid in Nicaragua and his suggestions about sources of information.

NAN WIEGERSMA
JOSEPH E. MEDLEY

1
Aid and Development

Introduction

Many Asian economies were gradually catching up to the 'First World' before the recent East Asian financial crisis slowed their growth. Most Latin American countries, after losing considerable ground in the 1980s, started to grow again in the 1990s. Africa, particularly sub-Saharan Africa, remains very poor and has continued to lose ground. After fifty years of successes and failures with economic development and development aid, what have we learned about the future possibilities for international cooperation, development and growth?

Following the remarkable successes of post-WWII reconstruction aid, 'First World' policy makers of the 1950s and early 1960s were optimistic about the possibilities of successful international help in promoting the development of less developed countries (LDCs). The US New Deal reform policies pursued in Japan, South Korea and Taiwan worked reasonably well to construct and set the basis for the advancement of economies which started at, in the cases of Taiwan and Korea, low levels of development. Starting with the Cold War politics of the Eisenhower administration, however, political-economic transformations within the United States fundamentally altered foreign aid policy. Cold War policies essentially changed the conditions and complexion of foreign development aid by directing US aid to preserve, and even increase, inequality between nations and between socioeconomic classes within nations.

Previous to the Cold War, there was a long-term historical connection between the development of capitalist markets and liberal-
democratic forms of government. Capitalism and political
democracy developed side by side in Europe and North America and
this same process was expected to occur in the 'Third World' with
the defeat of colonialism. With the advent of the Cold War,
however, foreign assistance spending, particularly military assistance, supported groups in power which opposed liberal-democratic
processes and showed little respect for civil liberties.

The governments of Taiwan and South Korea are a case in point.
In the case of East Asian development, widespread involvement in
the fruits of economic development proved to be sufficient for rapid
growth of capitalist markets to continue from the 1960s to the
1980s with very slow development of the institutional foundations
of liberal democracy and civil liberties. In Taiwan, progress in developing the democratic process was associated with Chiang Ching
Kuo's death, with the aging of the mainland coterie and with the
cumulative impact of women's, environmental, independence and
labor groups. In Korea, labor and student movements pressed for
and won democratic reforms. The slackening in US military and
police support in the post-Cold War era were additional factors in
accounting for the greater success of democratic forces in the 1990s.

Soon after the policy shift away from the New Deal, in the early
1960s, the Alliance for Progress, which was a Kennedy initiative for
development in the Western hemisphere, began. Few development
practitioners clearly understood the full implications of the new
Cold War policy change for development assistance. Although
small-scale egalitarian projects, including some limited land reform
and cooperative projects, were initiated during the 1960s in Latin
America, the overall policy direction incorporated regressive Cold
War support for existing elites. That is, most development aid went
towards, and directly benefitted, the traditionally powerful aristo-
cratic ruling classes. These elites were not particularly interested in
the social changes which are the necessary concomitants of growth
and development.

In practice, regressive Cold War policies meant that: (i) more
loans as opposed to grants were given in the 1960s, especially to
Latin America; (ii) less aid was given than in the reconstruction
period; and (iii) development and military aid were mixed in aid

packages justified almost entirely on their national security effects. Many of the countries receiving aid in the 1960s grew despite the biased structure of aid because world trade was booming and most of the world's economies were expanding. In countries like Vietnam and the Philippines, however, the problems with economic stagnation and weaknesses in US aid policy became quite apparent by the mid-1960s.

Vietnam posed a major challenge to Cold War political and military policies but economic development policies were not the focus of debate. By the beginning of the 1970s, debate about United States foreign policy centered on mistakes concerning the war in Vietnam rather than considering the overall problems with US economic interventions and development aid.

The dual crises of energy and debt dominated discussions of economic development during the remainder of the Cold War period, the 1970s and 1980s. Developing countries' export revenues were absorbed by rising oil costs and by the service charges on their tremendous debts. In the early 1980s recession in the developed countries slowed demand for developing country exports and thus exacerbated their economic development crises. It is unfortunate that the powerful and interconnected effects of these crises drew attention away from previously successful development and aid policies which continued to promote growth in the East Asian region. It is ironic that the development 'success stories' instituted during the New Deal era were not noted as they continued in spite of the development disasters that plagued their less successful counterparts.

Aid to less developed countries was very unevenly distributed in the Cold War period for concrete reasons. The two main drivers of bilateral economic development aid were the containment of Communism, for the United States, and the establishment of commercial networks, for Japan. It is important, although seldom acknowledged, that these two countries – the largest bilateral aid donors in the region – chose to focus on developing the same countries, Taiwan and South Korea, in the same region, East Asia. Although each was acting for their own particular reasons, the result was that East Asian development received an incredible boost. Meanwhile, Latin America received much less concessional aid and was given far less access to developed country markets – predictably, this region enjoyed little success compared to East Asia during this period.

Our analysis of aid successes, which includes examples from both East Asia and Latin America, emphasizes policy choice and institution-building while still recognizing the role of culture in constituting a growth-oriented set of practices. Some common explanations of the rapid development of East Asian countries (for example, Borthwich 1992) ignore the powerful effects of socioeconomic institutions, policy choice and aid and fall into a kind of 'cultural determinism' which attributes the success of the East Asian countries to benefits associated with Asian culture in general or the 'Confucian ethic' in particular. In a similar mode to analyses in which the 'protestant ethic' (Weber, 1980) has in the past been used to explain Western European development, this kind of analysis of development is, at best, partial. Our approach stresses, instead, the conditions for successful development which are multifaceted and can be established in many varied locales with differing sociocultural contexts.

Theories of stagnation and dependency

Theories of 'dependent development' were formulated in the 1960s and 1970s to explain continuing underdevelopment and inequality in the LDCs (Frank 1967; Baran 1957; Amin 1976; Bernstein 1982). According to these political economists, development which benefitted the mass of population in LDCs would be profoundly inimical to the dominant interests in the developed countries. In particular, Frank argued that, not only did developed countries block development in the LDCs, but that their own development also required the *underdevelopment* of the LDCs. The central contention of these 'dependency theorists' was that low-priced food, natural resources, and manufactured goods exports from the LDCs transferred value to the developed countries. The LDCs depend on the wealthy countries for the means to extract and produce these exports and for the markets in which to sell them, but lack the power to insist on beneficial terms of trade. Consequently, trade-mediated transfers of wealth promote growth in the wealthy recipient countries and reduce and deform it in the poor, donor countries. In this view, development traps LDCs in a poverty-stricken, subordinate position in the world economy.

Widespread and persistent poverty in much of the Third World seemed to support dependency theories and to controvert procapitalist modernization theory. However, rapid economic growth and extensive export-based industrialization in the newly industrializing countries (NICs) of East Asia, especially South Korea and Taiwan, were increasingly cited more recently as evidence that capitalist competition and 'getting prices right' in the capitalist world market is the key to successful development (Balassa 1981; Lal and Rajapatirana 1987). Anne Krueger (1997) argues that by the mid-1990s there existed a consensus among economists in support of these free-market views on development. Arnold Harberger elucidated these views (in his Presidential Address-Ely Lecture to the 1993 Allied Social Science Associations (1993a)). Even politically liberal theorists like Paul Krugman (1993) continued to argue that free-trade, free-market policies are the best possible ones and, consequently, read Taiwan's history in that light.

Some politicians, especially in the Reagan administration, claimed that the successes of the NICs supported the case for complete worldwide adoption of free-market policies. These politics (due to US efforts) influenced multinational agencies, including the World Bank and the International Monetary Fund (World Bank 1993). As a result, policies towards less developed countries were substantially redirected. The debt crises of the 1980s provided the opportunity for the International Monetary Fund/World Bank and bilateral donors to implement structural adjustment programs (SAPs). These established a set of international rules which favored restrictive monetary policy and a minimal role for the state. Specific adjustments included: (i) currency stabilization through tight money policies; (ii) reduced government spending on social services in order to balance budgets; (iii) privatization of government run firms; and (iv) export promotion through trade liberalization in order to produce shared development. Nevertheless, in the almost two decades since their enforcement, SAPs have produced no unqualified development success stories. Structural adjustment policies have often reduced budget and trade deficits, and in many cases they have reduced inflation, but they have not led to sustained economic growth with equity.

The East Asian challenge to structural adjustment

Despite a poor economic performance in the 1990s, Japanese economic development is certainly the most notable success story of the second half of the twentieth century. In this context, Japanese officials and scholars have vigorously joined the debate about appropriate development policies and the role of free markets. Important success stories, Taiwan and South Korea, are deeply integrated into Japan's production and trade system. In particular, they are major importers of Japanese technology and goods, sites of much subcontracting for Japanese producers and trade substantial volumes of goods via Japanese trading companies. A series of scholarly articles (Amsden 1979; Hart-Landsberg 1979; Hamilton 1983; Wade 1984) and some more recent, longer critical studies (Gold 1986; Amsden 1989; Alam 1989; Bello & Rosenfeld 1990; Wade 1990; Burris 1992) demonstrate that Taiwan, South Korea and other East Asian 'tigers' owe their economic development much more to important institutional factors than to free-market capitalism. The East Asian model involves substantial integration of participating Third World countries into a Japanese-dominated system. The Japanese have pressured the World Bank and the IMF to more explicitly draw development lessons from the East Asian experience (Prowse 1993). In the early 1990s the second most powerful country in the World Bank/IMF, Japan, became an increasingly important force for challenging the structural adjustment focus of these agencies. It is ironic that East Asia in the late 1990s has been so directly affected by these same policies.

Japan requested an extensive study from the World Bank of the East Asian development model to consider its feasibility as an alternative to the orthodox model. The report produced by that study, the *East Asian Miracle*, has strongly associated 'shared growth' or egalitarian distribution of the benefits of growth with the success of the East Asian economies. The report tentatively points to the importance of the development of human resources for East Asian growth. In her work outside the report, coauthor Nancy Birdsall takes the position that improvements in human welfare constitute development success and investments in education and health lead to economic development and growth (Birdsall 1992). The direction of causality between social and human resource development policies and economic development are not so clearly drawn out in the *East Asian Miracle*. Additionally, the study seems to downplay, and in its summary forms even to deny, the positive role development planning, resource redistribution (e.g., US-supported land reform), economic aid and privileged access to markets played in the development success of South Korea and Taiwan. On the other hand, a study of the degree of equality in the distribution of income and land ownership by Rodrik (1994) shows a significant correlation with growth rates for the high performing East Asian countries. These countries were compared with other countries at similar levels of economic development in 1960. The study shows significant correlations of growth with income equality and the levels of health and education. The most striking association, however, is between growth and land equality.

Despite the tentative tone of the *East Asian Miracle*, there are hopeful signs concerning the long run influence of the East Asian model in Washington. Recently, a proposal for a post-'Washington Consensus', in reaction to the East Asian financial crisis and the IMF response to the crisis, has been introduced by the chief economist of the World Bank, Joseph Stiglitz (Stiglitz 1998). Such a high-level official recommending substantial change from the structural adjustment model (the so-called 'Washington Consensus') shows the magnitude of problems with the results of the old ideas concerning privatization and liberalization. Stiglitz criticizes privatization for its own sake, as in Russia, where it did not enhance competition and efficiency. His main arena of critique, however, concerns the reverse effects of liberalizing financial regulations in East Asia on the overall health of the economies there. For example, he cites Thailand's bank liberalization which led directly to a real estate bubble that, when it burst, swamped the otherwise fairly healthy export economy. In support of a post-'Washington Consensus' policy, Stiglitz emphasizes the importance of stability through well-designed regulation, instead of deregulation, of effective financial markets (Stiglitz 1998a: 13–20).

Although the World Bank, in the *East Asian Miracle*, acknowledged that government policies encouraged industrial growth in some East Asian countries, the authors argued that governments cannot now be expected to achieve the same level of disciplined policy implementation as in Taiwan and Korea and that therefore the unregulated market would be preferred to government involvement in development planning. We disagree with the Bank's interpretation of Taiwan and Korea's economic histories – especially with respect to the role and extent of domestic and foreign government policy. We agree, instead, with the extensive critical responses to the World Bank's *East Asian Miracle* published in *World Development* (1994) and by Robert Wade in *Miracle or Design?* (1994). These articles show that the World Bank's own data controvert their report's laissez-faire conclusions and instead indicate that pervasive and effective state and foreign interventions successfully promoted economic growth with equity in East Asia.

In our earlier work (Medley 1989, 1994; Wiegersma 1988, 1994) we have argued the fundamental importance of egalitarian resource distribution (through land reform) and the significance of foreign aid and access to developed country markets. In this book, we show that Korea and Taiwan's economic histories prove just how tough it is to establish capitalist production and markets that lead to real benefits for most of the populace. We show that extensive interventions and management of production and markets is necessary to begin to realize potential benefits. We demonstrate the importance of US and Japanese aid, trade advantages and land reform support to East Asian development. Our book shows that Taiwan, South Korea and, later, Costa Rica received large amounts of grant aid which they used effectively. Their aid situations were special cases whose special characteristics promoted development. We then compare this successful set of policies to the post-Truman Cold War aid policy of the United States, which generally supported landowning elite classes and did not promote industrial development that shared the benefits of growth across society.

Evaluating the effectiveness of aid funding

A complete assessment of aid programs must look at the macroeconomic impacts of aid and at the changes in direction of other less developed countries' government funds caused by aid funding. The World Bank report's interpretation of the effectiveness of aid focuses on project-level evaluations. This evaluation technique indicates largely positive, but limited, benefits from aid. But this type of assessment does not account for the overall impact of projects on an economy through growth linkages.

Cross-country time series statistical analyses developed by the World Bank and the OECD (Organization of Economic Cooperation and Development) and independent authors such as Gupta and Islam (Gupta and Islam 1983; OECD 1992) have shown either negative or only slightly positive growth impacts from aid donations. However, these studies tend to add together the very few successful aid programs with the many unsuccessful cases to come out with a false 'average' situation. These studies also rarely account for the heterogeneity of aid: for example, a dollar spent on child nutrition is not equal to a dollar spent on police security (Cassen 1994: 14).

A sizable literature (e.g., Payer, 1982) argues the negative case. Since aid frequently came with strings attached, usually generated high repayment costs and went to the wrong people, it reproduced repressive power structures, sapped growth, and produced benefits for only a few in many recipient countries. As Griffin (1989: 82, 230) indicates, often aid does have adverse effects, or it is so small that its net effects are marginal. He also points out, however, that studies show positive effects of aid, *under the right conditions*. White (1992) points out that studies do show a net positive correlation between aid and growth. In fact, when aid reduces budget and foreign exchange constraints it is often associated with growth.

A country study analysis by the International Center for Economic Growth (Lele and Nabi 1991) suggests that money spent on projects without effective overall links to programs is wasted. Nevertheless, funds directed toward countries with development program leadership show positive returns. Another interesting result of this study is that the stability and consistency of aid flows and increased production and trade in manufactured goods are both important long-run determinants of development success. This study concludes that the transfer of technology and capital from developed to underdeveloped countries is best achieved by providing access to developed country markets. In other words, in order to better facilitate development, developed countries should reduce trade barriers and restrictions on technological transfer.

A recent World Bank study (World Bank 1998) found that both (1) economic policy and (2) institutional constraints heavily influence the overall success of economic aid. We thoroughly agree with this generalization. In contrast to the Bank's emphasis on market processes, we emphasize the importance of an institutional foundation that supports equitable distribution of property, power and income in the countries studied. The World Bank supports a policy of trade liberalization which forces LDCs to abandon their domestic industries while increasing exports of agricultural products and raw materials. We, on the other hand, demonstrate the importance of state support for import substituting industry as a precursor to export-led industrialization contingent upon access to developed country markets for trade expansion.

Super-exploitation of women industrial workers

Studies on the role of women in the industrialization of East Asian economies have suggested that women's hard work and low wages have been the backbone of development in East Asian nations. Because women workers are so oppressed in these countries and because patriarchal state policy keeps women in a particularly disadvantaged position, investment in these countries looks relatively attractive to international investors (Gallin 1990). East Asia is not exceptional in this process. Many countries, including the United States, began industrialization with young, unmarried women in textile and garment factories. These young females received a fraction of prevailing male wages, as they did in Korea in the 1970s and 1980s (Seguino 1994). Women workers are often the first industrial workers in each developing country; their pay is always low and their working conditions are invariably poor.

An important question about the role of women workers in the process of successful capitalist development is whether women workers ever benefit from, as well as contribute to, development. Recent research shows that on account of their own concerted efforts, organization and struggle as part of the Korean labor movement, women did benefit from industrial development in Korea (Seung-Kyung Kim 1992). As development has progressed in urban areas, women have moved into permanent jobs in the service sector (Seguino 1994). In addition, our analysis of Korean agricultural cooperatives in Chapter 3 shows that an increasing shortage of workers in the countryside led to increased wages for women agricultural workers.

The process of industrialization in many countries has depended on the exploitation of women workers and this is not a peculiarity of East Asia, nor is it a sufficient condition for its success. The use of an initial labor force of young, unmarried female workers is a generalized trend in nineteenth- and twentieth-century capitalist development. We argue that, depending on the policies chosen and on the institutions created, women may either be especially oppressed by capitalist industrialization or able to struggle effectively to extend their social roles, rights and welfare.

The special role of technology in late industrialization

The East Asian mode of obtaining and adapting technology is a fundamental factor in the development of the NICs. In fact, Alice Amsden (1989) has gone so far as to describe the developmental process in East Asia as 'development by learning'. East Asian countries have developed by adopting technology from the US and Japan. Innovation continued after the initial introduction of foreign technology. Persistent technological advance was possible because of a unique production system which empowers and rewards the engineering and technological know-how located on the shop floor. Technological knowledge is stored close to the production process in East Asia and the technological workers have, correspondingly, more decision making power than is common in the West.

This process of improvement and innovation located close to the production process will likely continue despite the financial crises of the late 1990s and the dire predictions from the left and the right that East Asian dynamism has run its course (Bello and Rosenfeld 1990; Petri 1995). We will describe how the East Asian economies have integrated into the international capitalist system and we will show why we think that these countries will continue to be successful.

Critics have pointed out that East Asian development has often imposed heavy costs on workers and the environment. Low pay for some workers, particularly women workers, along with long hours (between 50 and 54 hours a week) has led to labor unrest and organizing for higher wages. Chemically dependent agriculture and polluting industry have harmed the soil, air and waters in East Asia. Nevertheless, environmental movements have arisen which have struggled to set limits on both agricultural and industrial pollution and they have set goals for sustainable development. Our contention is that, despite the current crises, East Asian countries will deal more or less well with these ongoing labor, environmental and financial problems in much the same way that other developed capitalist countries have.

Can late entrants into industrial markets follow a technological frontier which is continuously moving? We argue that they can. Taiwan and Korea, like Japan before them, have been engaged in increasing the technological sophistication of their manufactured products as they adapt products to their own conditions. For the majority of products, however, East Asian producers have developed the capacity to quickly and closely follow new innovations developed elsewhere. They also take advantage of divisions in the production process of many products. For example, very advanced technology in textile production makes it cost-effective for Taiwanese companies to produce in Taiwan, ship their textiles to Nicaragua, have garments sewn there and then export them to the United States market.

World Bank economists have criticized the NICs for their institutional structure and suggested that they are in imminent danger of not being able to continue on a rapid growth path. Government involvement in the Korean economy, for example, has been seen as a limiting factor for potential growth. According to World Bank advisors, industrial policy should be adjusted by disengaging the government from managing the economy's structural development. Governments should simply coordinate and should avoid ad hoc policy measures. Some World Bank economists also believe that allocational issues, in terms of income and wealth distribution, should be left to private market forces (Leipziger and Petri 1993: 34–6). It would be hard to imagine the NICs voluntarily abandoning the bases of their development success in order to conform to World Bank or IMF preferences for a limited role of government and an enhanced role of the market in allocational decisions. We think that the governments of East Asian countries will continue wherever possible to be active in industrial policy and allocational decisions.

An alternative model

Research and analysis suggests that economic aid can make a significant contribution to development when it is in the form of grants and supplemented with extensive access to developed country markets. Success is also more likely if the country receiving aid has an institutional foundation which emphasizes the development of human resources and promotes an equitable distribution of resources and incomes. Support for thoroughgoing land reform in Japan, Korea and Taiwan was a central institutional factor in the 'New Deal' aid model. Once an egalitarian framework was established, the United States allowed East Asian planners to develop approaches which put their own socioeconomic development needs first.

This largely progressive and productive system of aiding agricultural and industrial development was abandoned by the US with a reversal of foreign aid policy in the late 1950s. In a 'Cold War' model, US aid policies were directed to benefit the power elites in Vietnam and in Central America and they opposed the needs of the broader population. The Cold War model of development assistance – developed in Vietnam, and extended in El Salvador, Honduras and Nicaragua and elsewhere – supported the native landed aristocracy and enforced the opening of domestic markets at the expense of nascent industries. These policies have proven to be remarkably unsuccessful in fostering industrialization with income equity. Political dependency and upper-class addiction to foreign aid have often been established instead of self-reliant capitalist development (Ryrie 1995: 48–50 and 114). Only in the Costa Rican aid program (1980–93) did this policy vary. In that exceptional case, the policy successfully promoted development because Costa Rica's pre-existing social-democratic institutions compelled an approach closer to the New Deal model employed in East Asia. Because of the presence of progressive institutional foundations and because the Costa Rican government was able to capitalize on their own (relative) independence, US-sponsored aid and trade benefits protected Costa Rica from the worst effects of the 1980s Latin American debt crisis.

In the present era, the policies of United States foreign aid are bound closely to the World Bank and IMF structural adjustment programs (SAPs). As explained above, these policies misconstrue East Asian success. SAPs are a way of continuing the 1980s Reagan–Bush–Thatcher realignment of power in favor of international capitalists as against labor and small domestic business in countries around the world. These reforms are undertaken in the name of the free market and the greater efficiency which is purported to come from

market-oriented systems. The outward-oriented (export-push) policies of the rapidly industrializing East Asian countries, however, are
not truly liberal, free-market reforms of their former import-substitution policies, because these outward-oriented programs are integrated parts of their governments' current development plans,
which are market-shaping, as well as market-conforming. The World
Bank/IMF SAPs favoring trade liberalization, privatization and cutbacks in government services have often disadvantaged lower classes
while advantaging (particularly international) capitalists. These
changes involve shifts in power in favor of international capitalists
and against domestic capitalists and workers. The following chapters
will show that these SAP reforms are very different from the institutional transformations that provided the basis for development in
East Asia.

Chapter 2 of this book traces the impact of United States interventionist policy in East Asia and the history of the shift to a Cold War
policy. Long-run trends in the overall developments of aid policy
are described and the political movement to eliminate US bilateral
aid is put into the perspective of long-term decreases in US commitments. The story of aid policy in Korea and Taiwan follow, with
emphasis on US support of land reform, agricultural development
and cooperatives in the countryside. Next, there is a description of
the US aid contribution to the early development of Korean and
Taiwanese industrial development and their subsequent integration
into the world capitalist economy. The concrete program and policy
differences between these commitments and Cold War interventions are then described. The story of US intervention in Vietnam is
assessed as an example of changing Cold War politics and negative
results from these changes. Closely following this experience were
similar policies and programs established in El Salvador in the
1980s. The contradictions underlying Cold War policies were high-
lighted most markedly in the small, under-developed country of
Nicaragua under the Sandinistas, as this county attempted in vain to
follow social-democratic policies which were in many ways less
radical than programs that the US had vigorously supported in an
earlier period in East Asia.

The Costa Rican 'difference' is then explored as we describe how
this small country, largely unnoticed by the United States, was able
to develop their own form of social-democratic institutional con-

struction in the 1950s and 1960s. With a relatively strong native elite in charge of the development process before US interventions began in the 1980s, the Costa Ricans were able to preserve a more autonomous development process.

Finally, we draw out lessons from the experience of US aid for the development of aid policies and programs in the modern era. The importance of institutional transformation, human development and access to markets and technology for future planning of aid agencies is emphasized in this concluding chapter. Factors with impede development and factors which accelerate development are delineated. No developing country will take exactly the same path as those that have gone before. Nevertheless, by comparing the successful development of Taiwan and Korea – through industrialization and increased export strategies – with the success of Costa Rica – which is based more on the production of nontraditional products and services, like tourism – we show some of the variety of successful capitalist development paths.

2
Successes and Failures: US Aid in the Postwar Era[1]

Introduction

This chapter will first explore the factors in United States development aid policy which helped set the course for the economic advancement of South Korea and Taiwan, utilizing the same model that had been established in Japan. Subsequently, a transformation of US foreign policy that occurred during the Eisenhower administration reversed this trend. This reversal was part of the Cold War redirection of policy away from New Deal antifascism and toward containment of communism through alliance with native elites in Third World countries. The United States no longer pushed for redistribution of property and power through land reform in its affiliate states. Instead, it placed itself squarely on the side of the power elites in Vietnam and Central America. These countries therefore lacked the modifying and democratizing element of large redistributive land reforms which had set the course for the earlier East Asian successes.

In later chapters of this book we will show how the help which the United States was able to give Taiwan and South Korea in the early stages of their development was important to their later success. By contrast, subsequent chapters demonstrate how the interventionist economic policies adopted by the United States in Vietnam in the 1950s and in El Salvador and Honduras in the 1980s were doomed to fail because they did not address issues which would have produced a successful process of economic development. In order to put the two very different sets of policies into

16

sharp relief, this chapter will outline United States postwar foreign economic policy interventions starting with policies toward Japan, Korea and Taiwan and then continuing with those in Vietnam and Central America.

In Japan, South Korea and Taiwan, the US supported thorough-going land reforms with low retention limits (approximately 3 hecrares) and then offered help with national development projects, but they limited further political interference with economic development planning. The other model of intervention, which was used in Vietnam in the 1950s and 1960s, El Salvador in the 1980s and Nicaragua in the 1990s, supported the native landed aristocracy. This support was also conditioned upon interference with the details of economic policy and the replication of US forms of capitalist institutions in these countries. These policies are especially associated with the Cold War foreign interventionist politics of Eisenhower in the 1950s and Reagan in the 1980s. Nevertheless the Democratic and Republican presidents in the intervening period had only limited effects in changing this general policy direction.

The New Deal in Asia

In Japan, Korea and Taiwan, a 'New Deal' was generated after World War II which was related to similar politics in Franklin Delano Roosevelt's US New Deal. According to Theodore Cohen (1987), a participant in MacArthur's occupation of Japan, the direction of radical reform in Asia was provided by the experience of the US New Deal. Along with political democracy, there was a tendency to widen the ownership of the economy through land reform and the dismantling of large corporations. The underlying purpose of these reforms was to ward off communism. The New Deal method of competing with communism was the opposite of the Cold War method. The emphasis was on providing for the basic economic well-being for the lower classes. In this respect, the New Deal for Japan, Korea and Taiwan was specifically an economic and not a political New Deal. Cohen makes this clear when he states that Japanese unions should be 'economic unions', disconnected from left-wing political movements in the country (ibid.: 40). The non-political, economistic, nature of the formula for economic success, however, was taken even further in Japan than similar politics were in the US. A series of strikes called by more militant and political leaders eventually led to a political compromise with the Nationalist Party in power whereby workers job security in major industries would not be sacrificed but there would be no industry-wide unions (Borthwick 1992: 244). Only a system of nonfederated company unions bargaining on economic issues were allowed.

The key issue, from the perspective of the New Dealers in Japan, was the distribution of ownership of production and trade. The *Zaibatsus*, large industrial groups, were broken up (only to recombined after the Americans left) and peasant and worker organizations were encouraged to form around limited economic demands. The New Dealers saw themselves as having to provide a realistic alternative to the communists as the fascists were driven out of power.

Wolf Ladejinsky was a strongly anticommunist Russian émigré New Dealer in charge of agrarian reform in Japan. He had accepted the post-World War II lessons where the Baltic states and Rumania had demobilized radical movements by offering a program of land reform. There was also the alternative lesson of a successful radical movement closer at hand in Asia – the 1949 Revolution in China. Ladejinsky described Asia as 'a continent where agrarian discontent is gnawing at the vitals of the social order. It is on this strife that the communists have been able to capitalize so successfully ...'(Ladejinsky 1977: 130). At the end of the war, there were few large landlords remaining in the Japanese countryside. The remaining landlords would be helped in their transitions to an urban environment, or helped in their old age, with payments for their former property with the new land reform.

Under these conditions, Ladejinsky developed the Japanese land reform law, thus beginning a tradition of American formulation of land reform laws of other countries in the postwar period. What Ladejinsky had in mind was a thoroughgoing redistribution of wealth in the countryside without fundamental changes to the political economy. This was made possible by continuing tenancy as an institution peripheral to ownership. Ladejinsky thought that complete abolition of tenancy was neither feasible nor desirable. Although owner-farmers increased from around 40 to 70 per cent with the reform, a large percentage of farmers still rented some land from other families in the villages (ibid.: 69). Ladejinsky had studied the interwar period of Japanese landlord–tenant relations. He knew of the extensive development of tenant unions in Japan in that period – when unions represented a quarter of all tenant farmers – and he also knew of the open conflicts between landlords and tenants (ibid.: 81). Furthermore, he was clear in his view that the major issue which had arisen with market development in Japan was security of tenure. No matter how oppressive the rents, the most important issue to the Japanese farmer was one which had arisen with Western-style rental contracts. The length of tenure in these contracts was specified as from three to five years, at the end of which the renter could be arbitrarily removed. This issue, more than the level of exploitation, had radicalized the Japanese peasantry. By making the great majority of Japanese peasants owners of their cropland, Ladejinsky took away much of the insecurity. Where security of tenure was no longer as important because enough land for basic survival was owned, families often rented some additional land.

Ladejinsky described the New Deal reforms he helped to develop in Japan as a middle-class revolution designed to create a stable system of democratic capitalism. The security of tenure in agriculture and rights to labor security in industry were important foundations of this reconstructed capitalist system. Ironically, this style of capitalism developed by American policies with income security for the majority of workers and peasants would prove to be so successful that it would become a challenge to US capitalism in a later period. Ladejinsky went on to visit Taiwan and help to formulate the same type of land reform that had been established in Japan. The peasants would secure their tenures through purchasing their land in a long term mortgage-type arrangement. Although Ladejinsky was not directly involved with the Korean reform, that reform also secured tenures for the peasants in a real estate transaction style of reform.

By the time that the US became involved in another intervention in Asia, in the 1950s in Vietnam, the global political climate had changed, ardor for the New Deal had cooled and the developmental aspects of US interventions were reversed. Thoroughgoing land reform could thenceforth not be a part of future interventions. United States interventionary policy changes were a result of shifts in US international policy and a shift from the Truman to the Eisenhower administrations. Many of the New Dealers in government service who had been appointed during the Roosevelt administration, and had survived during the Truman era, were replaced during the Eisenhower years. Ladejinsky's politics and his 'security problems' were brought into question by Secretary of Agriculture Benson in 1955. In early 1956 he was asked to resign supposedly because of a personal investment he had made in a factory in Taiwan (Hanson 1957: 155).[2] The 1949 Korean Land Reform was enthusiastically sponsored and promoted by the United States. The land reform in Taiwan – which was prepared in late 1951 and 1952, but not carried out until 1953–4 – continued with massive US assistance. In 1952, Robert Hardie, who had served directly under Ladejinsky in Japan, developed proposals for a redistributive land reform in the Philippines. The president of the Philippines at the time rejected the proposal and by the time a new president was elected the next year, the United States had lost interest in supporting new land reform proposals (McCoy 1971: 28–9).[3] When the United States intervened in Vietnam in 1955, New Deal-style land reform was no longer a political possibility.

Establishment of the AID regime

At the end of World War II, among the big powers, only the United States remained unravaged by the war. The country was, in fact, in a better economic state than at the war's outset, since it had shaken off the last clouds of the Great Depression and it had also fostered renewed confidence in the power of US industry. With this new found strength, the US set about constructing a new political-economic world order through the Marshall Plan, with its first task being to rebuild Western Europe.

The United Nations Relief and Rehabilitation Agency (UNRRA) was the first major US aid program after World War II. It began almost immediately after the end of the war in response to the threat of mass starvation in many regions of Central Europe. The total destruction of the economic base throughout Europe and Asia left large portions of the population without access to basic subsistence commodities. The agency's charter was supposed to provide only those immediate relief needs which could not be met out of the resources of the countries involved. Economic problems were severe. Eberstadt (1985) has pointed out, for example, that Germany's infant mortality rate at the end of World War II was higher than Sub-Saharan Africa's was estimated to be in the 1980s. When the basic needs had been met, UNRRA was disbanded in 1947, having prevented mass famine in the war-torn nations.

A series of transfer projects affecting post war Western Europe, collectively known as the Marshall Plan, was then initiated under the European Recovery Act of 1947 and a similar program was initiated for Japan. This program focused on reconstruction of infrastructure and industrial plants and equipment destroyed during the war. During the four-year period from 1948 to 1951, $13 billion were disbursed in the form of grants and loans to Europe and Japan ($3.7 billion to the United Kingdom, $2 billion to Japan). The value of this assistance in today's terms has been estimated at $45 billion (Morse and Morse 1982: 19).

The Plan was never designed only to rebuild Western Europe – it always had a much grander goal. The underlying push was toward an international economy, reconstructed by the US with the intent of avoiding the economic downturns that policy makers saw as a cause of the Great Depression. In Keynesian interventionist fashion, the US government set about reconstructing the major national economies and also worked toward constructing a multilateral world economy based on the unobstructed movement of capital and labor. It is not difficult to understand why attention was initially concentrated on Europe. As the major US allies and largest trading partners, these economies were inextricably tied together. There was also the threat of the spread of communism and the need to realign the balance of power throughout Europe and in Asia. The end of World War II saw the dismantling of the overseas possessions of European colonial powers, such as France, Britain and the Netherlands. As the old economic order was coming to an end, the US stepped in, using the money distributed through the European Cooperation Administration (ECA). These funds went into Europe and then, in part, to their colonies. In this way the Marshall Plan helped to tie Europe, North America, and the Third World into a new economic integration.

Civil wars were being waged in Indochina and Malaysia and elsewhere against the reinsertion of colonial power. The United States, by providing large amounts of money to Europe, was in effect paying for the European nations' wars with their colonies. As these insurgencies evolved, the US began to play a more active role through helping Europe. These European alliances in this circumstance led the US into military interventions that have had major consequences throughout the post-World War II period.

The early linkages of aid programs with the Third World were not only through colonial ties; they also came through trade relations. The Third World had two major roles in the success of the Marshall Plan: firstly, it was the market for European goods, a market which had previously existed in the East and could not be replaced by suitable US demand. The second role of the Third World was that of exporter of raw materials to the US. The increasing demand by the United States for raw materials promised, in turn, to assist US private investment in the Third World. This basic triangular pattern of world trade was a keystone of the Marshall Plan: Europe exporting goods to the Third World, with exports by the Third World going to the US and exports by the US moving to Europe. In this way the United States established a hegemonic relationship over the new world market as it was being established.

As the Marshall Plan came to a close, the entire world's foreign aid machinery was dominated by the US since what little supplementary funds other countries contributed were underwritten by the United States. The Marshall Plan had been so successful by its close that aid planners were optimistic about including more ambitious tasks in aiding underdeveloped countries over the next several decades. In his 1949 State of the Union address President Truman outlined a 'Four Point Program' which was to allow less developed countries to benefit from the existing international economic updraft by fair access to resources and markets. The thrust of Truman's plan was to add technical assistance to the already established aid in support of infrastructural and manufacturing development which had been included in the Marshall Plan. As stated in the President's message to Congress, the assistance fell into two categories: (i) technical, scientific and managerial knowledge including resource surveys and planning and (ii) production goods, that is machinery and equipment, and financial assistance in the creation of productive enterprises (Truman 1973: 551). Truman recommended an initial appropriation of $45 million, to be expanded as required. Congress passed the Act for International Development in 1950 which gave legal basis to Truman's plan.

Eisenhower: from development aid to police security

The most important change in US aid policy in the postwar era was the shift from a strategy of fighting communism through land redistributions to peasants, to a program for establishing security for the existing elites in the form of military and police assistance. This profound change took place during the Eisenhower years (1952–60). Land redistribution programs such as Taiwan's, which had been started in 1951, still received the full support of the United States. As discussed earlier, the opportunity for US-supported land reform of the old type was barely missed in the Philippines, where the president in office rebuffed such an offer of support in 1952. By the time that a pro-land reform Philippine president was elected in 1954, the Eisenhower Cold War policy was in place and the US was no longer interested in pursuing such a policy. In Vietnam, the security of the landlords, not the peasants, was protected in the US-supported 1955 land reform. With landlord retention limits of 100 hectares, the US-sponsored reform took land which peasants had acquired through the Viet Minh and gave it back to the landlords. Thus, the land reform policy of the US shifted in a few years from land reform to 'reverse' land reform.[4]

The periods of change in post-Marshall Plan aid policy which have been considered important are: (i) Kennedy's Alliance for Progress; (ii) the post-1973 basic needs strategy following the US defeat in Vietnam; and (iii) the Reagan return to security aid. From a political perspective which looks at property and power, however, the most important shift in AID strategy was the shift to security aid during the Eisenhower years. Not only was land reform aborted after 1952, but also security aid worked toward the defeat of peasants organizing in their own interest since the elite now had effective weapons to put down peasant uprisings. Between 1949 and 1953, military grants and political aid for regimes friendly to the United States accounted for barely a sixth of foreign aid. Between 1953 and 1961, security aid increased to over half of the aid program (Eberstadt 1985: 23). The Mutual Security Act was passed in the early 1950s and the Mutual Security Agency was set up to take over the duties formerly carried out by the Economic Cooperation Agency. Economic assistance was subordinated to security assistance.

After World War II, the United States had taken on the obligation of helping its allies to recover and Truman's Four Point Program attempted to extend Marshall Plan- type aid to LDCs. The Eisenhower administration recognized no such obligation to support poor countries with economic aid. In 1954 the Randall Commission on Foreign Economic Policy stated that 'Underdeveloped areas are claiming a right to economic aid from the United States ... We recognize no such right.' The purpose of aid was very simply to fight Soviet communism and Eisenhower's 'modus operandi' for doing this was by cementing alliances and propping up existing regimes.

This conservative policy may have been aimed at preserving the status quo politically while promoting economic growth, but its results were quite different. Security aid fundamentally changed the dynamics of internal politics within poor countries. Not only was the existing class structure strengthened through military aid, police aid and covert activities favoring the upper classes, but there was also a shift in the balance of power toward the military and away from civilian leaders. Khaleque (1980: 92) explains these political effects of the security aid program on underdeveloped countries: 'In poor countries where political institutions are fragile and people are largely uneducated and unorganized, military equipment received through aid programs has given the soldiers an overwhelming advantage over civilians.'

The ideas about political security and economic growth and development which were later to be associated with Rostow's role in the Kennedy administration were actually put into effect much earlier. Walter Rostow and Max Miliken produced a study of the foreign aid program for the Senate in 1956. The main conclusion of the study was that economic aid promotes economic growth and therefore constitutes a weapon against communism. If only the security aid could hold down insurgency for long enough, then sustained growth would eventually occur and eliminate any further security problems (Rostow 1985: 42–8). The assumptions behind this analysis were that police and security aid was simply a stopgap and that economic assistance would automatically increase growth rates in less developed countries. It is ironic but understandable that under the conditions of poverty and insecurity of tenures for the peasantries of the Philippines and Vietnam, economic aid became

'no-growth' aid in the very same time period when Rostow first per-
suaded Congress to accept his analysis. Rostow (1985: 173ff, 207ff)
reflects that the aid initiatives fostered by his analysis of Latin
America and India, on the other hand, were more progressive than
strictly security aid without economic assistance would have been.

By 1954–5, aid to South Vietnam, $324 million in 1987 dollars,
had out-paced aid to any other country, including South Korea
($301 million) and Taiwan ($132 million) (see Figure 2.1). Although
aid to South Korea and Taiwan was reasonably effective in helping
with capitalist economic development, the large amounts of aid
going to South Vietnam succeeded only in building dependency
with no growth in per capita income (Wiegersma 1988: 173). Figure
2.1 shows that, although in real terms the year-to-year aid contributions to Vietnam were greater than those to South Korea, the South
Korean contribution promoted successful capitalist development
while the Vietnamese contribution did not.

The Food for Peace Program (PL 480) was first developed during
the Eisenhower administration. Although this program was unques-
tionably a boon to American farmers, its use in LDCs had mixed
results. The presence or lack of an effective land reform made an
essential difference in the receiving countries. In the case of South
Korean development, for example, the PL 480 food shipments were
used by the government to keep food costs, and therefore labor
costs, low during their industrialization process. Although lower
food prices were a disincentive for Korean farmers, these farmers by
and large did not have large rents to pay because of the land reform
and therefore they were able to develop. South Korean agriculture
continued to grow, albeit at a slower rate of growth than Korean
industry. On the other hand, in this same period of time, PL 480
shipments to Vietnam succeeded only in supporting a corrupt government that was increasingly separated and alienated from the
countryside.

Another trend in the aid program of the 1950s was the transition
from an overwhelming predominance of grants-in-aid to a much
higher reliance on loans. In the first few years of its operation,
Marshall Plan aid had been overwhelmingly (90 per cent) in the
form of grants. During the 1950s the percentage in loans increased
from approximately one per cent in 1952–3 to 35 per cent by l960–l
(White 1974: 207). Not only was a majority of this aid for military

26

Figure 2.1 US grants and credits to the Far East, 1945–90

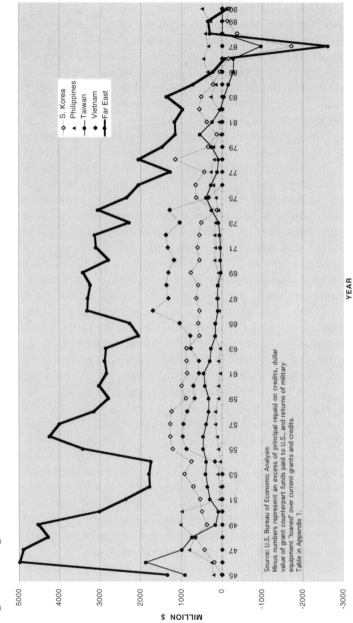

Source: U.S. Bureau of Economic Analysis
Minus numbers represent an excess of principal repaid on credits, dollar
value of grant counterpart funds paid to U.S., and returns of military
equipment 'loaned' over current grants and credits.
Table in Appendix 1.

and police security by the end of the decade and therefore not directed towards developmental projects, but Third World governments were also increasingly being asked to pay interest on the military equipment and police forces that were financed by loans from the United States. The US aid program had been set up in such a way that regimes could more easily abuse their power over their own people. In addition, governments were encouraged to incur increasing indebtedness which would eventually open the door to credit-driven adjustment/austerity programs.

Variations in Cold War policy

Kennedy's Alliance for Progress' first proposed in March 1961, was intended to be a bold new concept in aid that would change the face of the Americas in ten years. It advocated a policy of fending off the communist menace – or more specifically, the prospects of other countries in the Western Hemisphere going in the direction of Cuba – by putting together a large aid package and persuading the leaders of the various countries to become involved in planning development. The Peace Corps was a brilliant additional idea which tapped the idealism of youth in the US by sending them to poor countries to work on projects. With Kennedy's Alliance, the growth problems of the Americas were to be solved in the decade of the 1960. His proposal read: 'basic education will be available to all, hunger will be a forgotten experience, the need for massive outside help will have passed, most nations will have entered a period of self-sustaining growth' (Kennedy 1973: 660). Kennedy requested Congress to appropriate $394 million to the Inter-American Development Bank for 'soft' loans (i.e. loans in the LDC's own currencies), $6 million to the Organization of American States for planning grants and $100 million to the International Cooperation Agency (predecessor to USAID) and his requests passed through Congress in less than two months (ibid.: 661).

At the end of 1961, Kennedy abolished the existing aid agencies and constructed the Agency for International Development (USAID)', putting it under the control of the Department of State. This was a move consistent with the philosophy of the new aid package which suggested that developmental aid and security aid were closely connected. Funding and monitoring of police training and counterinsurgency was not separated out from agricultural research and local health projects. Aid had become a tool of foreign policy and the province of the Department of State.

Despite the hype surrounding the Alliance for Progress, the results of this huge effort were disappointing. Economic aid was supposed to automatically turn into higher growth rates – via Rostow's theory of stages of growth – but there were few concrete moves in the direction of a redistribution of resources which might spur growth as New Deal economics had in an earlier period. The idealistic conception of the Alliance was that it would support agrarian reform and a redistribution of resources but since the program operated through existing power elites, the implementation was quite different. There was mention of land reform in the Alliance proposal which suggested that the Alliance would attack 'archaic tax and land tenure systems.' Small farmer cooperatives were encouraged with US funding in Central America under the Alliance. USAID also supported unionization movements among agricultural workers and small-scale renters. Despite these efforts, however, the landed elites with governing power continued to receive support from Washington. Democratic freedom was an aim of the document but lack of political freedom was narrowly defined as the socialism in Cuba and the extreme repression under Trujillo in the Dominican Republic.

Despite the problem with security aid, there remained significant economic aid which could have had more developmental impact if not for other problems. Although the amount of economic aid sent to Latin America during the decade of the 1960s was almost ten times greater than military aid, the two types of aid could easily be substituted in the countries themselves (New Directions 1969: 11). When aid funds were used for a project that would have been carried out anyway by the host government, this government could more easily pursue greater military empowerment because of the aid funds. Thus, although the US increased the amount labeled economic aid in the decade of the 1960s compared to the 1950s, the US government tended to look the other way when funds were substituted.

Figure 2.2 shows that the increased aid to Latin America in the 1960s nevertheless remained well below the aid commitment to the Far East (East and Southeast Asia). Even on a real per capita basis, aid expenditures have been significantly lower to Latin America than to the less developed East and Southeast Asian countries (minus

Figure 2.2 US grants and credits to the Far East and Latin America, 1945–90

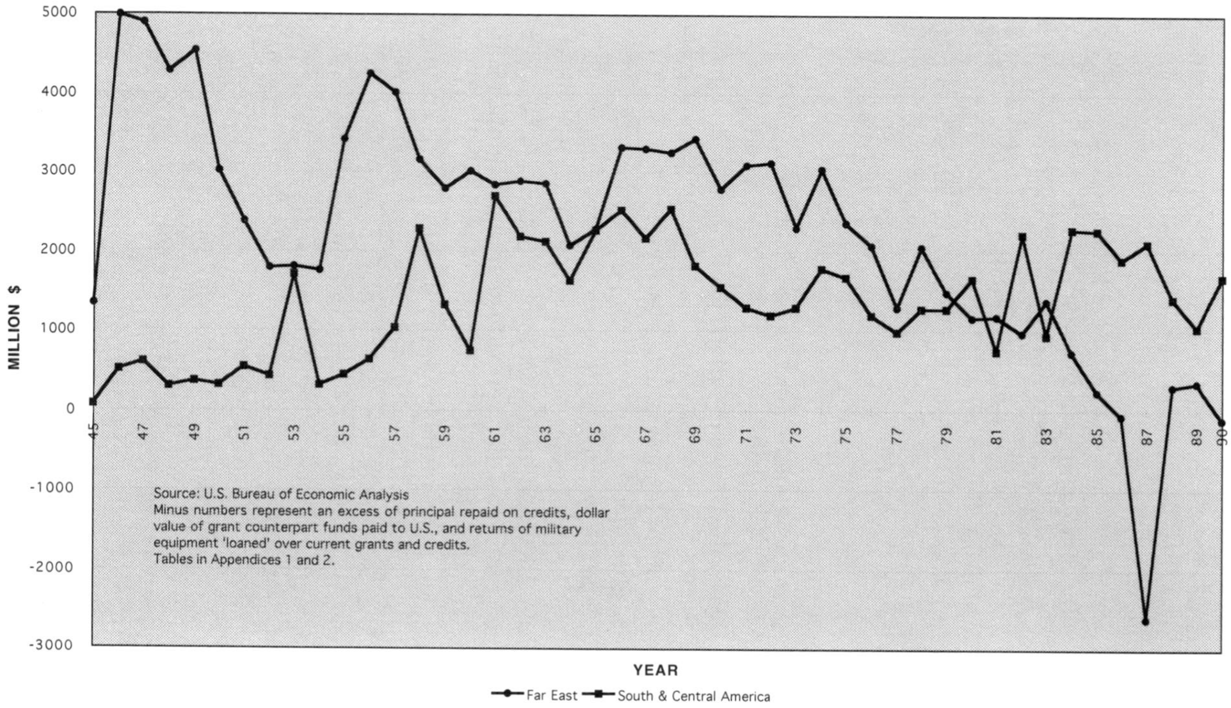
5000
4000
3000
2000
1000
0
-1000
-2000
-3000
MILLION $
45
47
49
51
53
55
57
59
61
63
65
67
69
71
73
75
77
79
81
83
85
87
89
90
Source: U.S. Bureau of Economic Analysis
Minus numbers represent an excess of principal repaid on credits, dollar value of grant counterpart funds paid to U.S., and returns of military equipment 'loaned' over current grants and credits.
Tables in Appendices 1 and 2.
YEAR
Far East
South & Central America

China) throughout most of the postwar period.[5] The threat of communism was significant enough in Asia following the Chinese revolution to pull larger amounts of aid funding to these further away locations.

The next significant change in aid legislation came in 1973 as a result of the disappointing results of the sixties development decade and the failure of the US efforts in Vietnam. In the early 1970s, policy makers in the US were noticing that aid to the elites in Latin America and elsewhere were not helping the poor and that the disparity of incomes in these countries was in fact becoming greater. Specific projects which would help rural subsistence farmers and others in poverty were supposed to be developed in the new Basic Needs Program. The international aid agencies followed this new direction.

The trend toward multilateralization of aid that began in the 1960s accelerated in the following decade. The World Bank, heavily influenced by the US, led the efforts to formulate an international aid policy. In 1973 under Robert McNamara, the Bank implemented the new policy of aid to meet basic needs. Nevertheless, when countries took loans in order to carry out anti-poverty projects that were not directly linked to production growth, a devastating problem arose. The anti-poverty projects tended to have positive, but partial results. They often alleviated some symptoms of poverty, but did not lead to production increases that were sufficient to pay off the loans. In the next decade and a half, because of international economic trends (for example, low prices for their primary product exports and high prices for energy) poorer countries had debt repayment problems that required assistance from the IMF. In order to pressure these countries to service their accumulated foreign debt before they attended to their domestic problems, the IMF imposed SAPs that required the countries to cut back more services in the 1980s than they had added in the 1960s and 1970s. Therefore, many underdeveloped countries ended up less able to meet their peoples' basic needs than when they started out with the World Bank programs.

As for the United States, the bilateral aid programs formulated under the Nixon administration during the 1970s tied economic aid to security aid. Thus, there was a basic conflict between Nixon's foreign policy and the Basic Needs approach. In a 1973 speech concerning the aid bill Nixon very frankly warned Congress about where his bias lay on this issue. He declared that aid was not just for altruistic purposes, but must also be for security purposes. United States bilateral aid in the early 1970s therefore maintained its Cold War security bias despite the currency of the Basic Needs philosophy.

President Carter, on the other hand, intensified efforts to realize the mandates of the Basic Needs approach. Carter removed USAID from direct State Department control and placed it under another agency called the International Development Cooperation Agency. In addition, he signed agreements for cutbacks of military and police security programs. He commissioned two studies of world poverty – the Presidential Commission on World Hunger and the Global 2000 studies. The Carter policy paid particular attention to problems of poverty in the poorest nations in the world, those in Africa. He pointed out later that solving problems of poverty was considered more important during his administration than the perceived anticommunist political litmus tests of African leaders that were common in the past (Wilkie 1990: 42–3). Unfortunately, his efforts to focus on economic problems in aid to Africa were quickly reversed during the Reagan era.

On the other hand, Carter's aid policy was not consistently liberal in Central America. In line with his liberal perspective, Carter had canceled aid to Guatemala because of human rights violations there. Although Carter continued a minimal aid program in Nicaragua after the Sandinista revolution, in an attempt to encourage Nicaragua not to ally with the Soviet Union, he had nevertheless supported the former leader, Somoza, as long as he had remained in power. With respect to his policy toward El Salvador the conservatives in his administration had the most influence and the Carter administration implemented a special security aid fund administered by the State Department, called the Economic Support Fund, in order to support the government in their war against the FMLN (Landes and Flynn 1984: 145). Reagan later quadrupled this fund and, in addition, reversed all of Carter's other, more liberal, policies in Central America.

Figure 2.3 shows that aid to Central America was insignificant until the Sandinista revolution of 1979. After the revolution, aid poured into the remaining Central American countries in large amounts. As with the Asian examples, however, large amounts of aid sent to El Salvador and Honduras on the one hand, and Costa

32

Figure 2.3 US grants and credits to Latin America, 1945–90

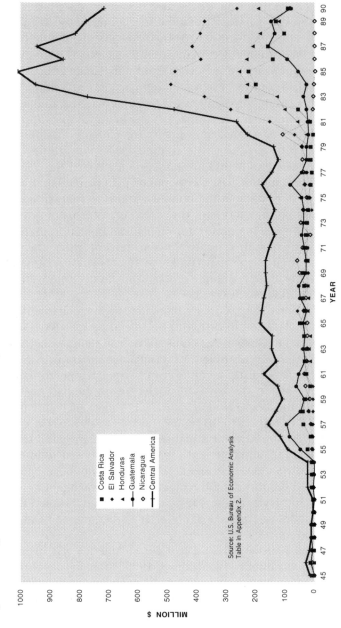

Rica on the other, had very different effects (as we will see in Chapters 6 and 7). Reagan completely reverted to the blatantly military and security aid concepts of the 1950s. Foreign political policy was clearly in the forefront and security-oriented loans and grants soon completely overshadowed development assistance. The cause of the Reagan administration's shift was a new philosophy of development which included a very limited role for development aid. Their philosophy was based on the belief that stimulation of international trade and increases in private investment in less developed countries would be the only route to take for successful economic development (Reagan 1984: 140–2).

The Export Economy Model promoted by the Reagan administration in Central America often used Taiwan and South Korea as examples of successful free-market development. These claims are ironic, since the help that the United States gave to these countries had been based on the politics of the New Deal while Reagan's policies were the opposite: a wholesale reversion to the Eisenhower strategy of fighting communism through supporting landlord elites in the Third World. Although Reagan's policies were as different as possible from the New Deal policies, he falsely claimed that the success that those earlier policies generated in South Korea and Taiwan were due to his own approach.

Conclusion

Looking through the lens of the politics and the class structure that aid supports shows the differences between the New Deal economic intervention strategy of supporting redistribution of resources to peasants in rural areas of less developed countries and the Eisenhower strategy of achieving 'mutual security' by supporting the distribution of power and wealth that exists in these countries. The New Deal in the United States provided the protection that workers needed in order to accept a reformed version of capitalism and the harmony that made a postwar development boom possible. The foreign policy 'New Deal' for Asian countries on the perimeter of communism included US political and economic support for redistribution of rural resources. This development provided a secure institutional foundation and cheap resources for industrialization in these countries.

Liberal or conservative policies under capitalism make a difference for people living in the developed world. The analysis in this chapter suggests that the difference has been much greater for people living in underdeveloped countries that fall under the sphere of influence of the United States. Those same 'archaic' class structures that the Alliance for Progress was supposed to challenge, but in many ways supported, have prevented development in the thirty years of 'mutual security' arrangements. Given the breakdown of the barriers of the Cold War, the present period should provide possibilities for changes similar to those pursued in Taiwan and Korea, and described in Chapter 3 and 4, to be adopted for countries outside East Asia.

Notes

1. For their historical research for this chapter we owe thanks to three students – John Kress, William Moser and David Nolan.
2. Marilyn Young (1991: 57) states that Ladejinski developed the Ordinance 57 (Diem) land reform. This is very unlikely since he was forced to resign from the Eisenhower administration nine months before the ordinance became law and the political position expressed in his 1955 Vietnam report favored a lot more redistributive efforts than occurred under Ordinance 57.
3. Al McCoy (1971) suggests that the reason for the change in US policy was that the political radicals, the Huks, had been defeated in the Philippines. He thinks that the clear and present danger of communism was the guiding factor with New Deal land reforms. The problem with this analysis is that there was a very real and present danger of communist success in Vietnam and yet the US-sponsored 'reform' strongly favored the landlords there.
4. Another example of 'reverse' land reform was in Guatemala in 1955. After the CIA organized a coup against Arbenz, who had carried out land reform, the newly installed military dictator, Colonel Armas, dismantled the Arbenz reforms according to David Landes and Patricia Flynn (1984: 136).
5. Communist China was, of course, not receiving aid from the US and aid to Japan had ceased. The Pacific Rim countries supported included Southeast Asia, with approximately the same population as Latin America, and also the East Asian countries of South Korea, Taiwan and Hong Kong. South East Asia, together with these less developed East Asian countries, had a population approximately 20 per cent greater than Latin America. However, real aid expenditure (in per capita terms) in most years in the Asian countries was much greater than in Latin America even taking. So, US aid to the Asian Pacific Rim was greater than aid to Latin America in the Cold War period in both absolute and per capita terms.

3
Agriculture in Taiwan and South Korea

Introduction

US economic and political policies and interventions supported materially beneficial development in Taiwan and South Korea. They were intended to serve as models of noncommunist, politically stable and economically successful societies operating with free-market institutions within the US sphere of influence. The generalization of their actual experience as a model of foreign-assisted, state-led development would, if replicated currently, be quite costly: politically, socially and economically. The following chapter will show that the actual model East Asian countries followed contrasts with the 'free-market' model that is currently touted by the US and international agencies. The East Asian model involves high direct costs associated with significant changes in class relations and extensive economic aid as well as high indirect costs associated with providing access to developed country (especially US) markets. In the geopolitical context of post-WWII East Asia, the US was willing and able to pay these costs to demonstrate the superiority of free-market institutions within the sphere of US influence. In more recent decades, however, the US and some international agencies have rewritten (reinterpreted) Taiwan and South Korea's experiences in order to avoid these costs by attributing their success to a 'free-market miracle.'

Taiwan and South Korea, in many respects, are exemplary cases of state-managed and foreign-assisted development. The United States, and the Taiwan and South Korean governments, in their own relatively independent ways and for their own purposes, planned these countries' integration into the US-dominated post-World War II international economy. The intersection of their efforts produced conditions that simultaneously promoted the internationalization of US capitalism throughout the Pacific Rim and strengthened Taiwan and South Korea's domestic economies.

US policy makers wanted a stable model of anticommunist development. Land reform, the promotion of peasant cooperative associations and related government interventions into Taiwan and South Korea's agricultural sectors produced positive results. They allowed the US to claim that these two countries are models of noncommunist, politically stable, 'free-market' economies. US policy in Japan, Taiwan and Korea reflected the ideology that redistribution and peasant ownership of resources could create a stable peasantry resistant to communism. The geographic requirements of bolstering an anticommunist alliance made the US willing to intervene to support interventionist government policies, to support major changes in class relations, and to sponsor the development of small, family farms linked together in agricultural cooperatives in order to support materially beneficial development in their agricultural sectors.

Dependent agricultural development and land reform

Economic development is difficult for smaller, agroexport-dependent countries like Taiwan and South Korea were in the mid-twentieth century. Economic growth requires, first of all, the production, appropriation, distribution and effective utilization of economic surplus for the development of infrastructure, social services and for investments in additional means of production. It is difficult, however, for private or even public agencies in less developed countries (LDCs) to generate and control much economic surplus. In addition, agroexport countries do not have the capacity to domestically produce many means of production or consumer goods at internationally competitive prices. Thus, they must produce and export traditional agricultural products or minerals in order to appropriate surplus in a form (i.e., foreign exchange) which would allow them either to construct a capacity for self-sufficient economic development or to pay for the imports necessary to sustain and expand production and consumption. Therefore, self-reliant economic development, much less autarkic development, is not usually a viable option.

Small LDCs are typically integrated into the international economy as exporters of agricultural or other primary products. Their exports generate the revenue to pay for their imported means of production and consumer goods required to continue export production. Their level of production and trade is based, in part, upon extreme exploitation (poor working conditions, long hours, low wages, few services, etc.) of their labor force, in order to create the low unit costs which enable internationally competitive export prices. Export production is also often dependent upon external finance, technology, transport and markets (Fitzgerald 1986). Integration into the international economy can create an uneven, mutual dependency between these nations and their larger, more economically advanced, counterparts.

Dependent agricultural development in Taiwan and Korea

Taiwan in 1949 was a poor nation. As Japan's colony, Taiwan's social structure was modified and directed toward producing basic agricultural goods, predominantly sugar and rice, in order to export high quality, low-cost food to Japan. Most people in Taiwan did not own land or work in steady, well-paid jobs. In prewar Taiwan the top 10 per cent of landholders controlled about 60 per cent of the land, while the bottom 40 per cent held approximately 5 per cent (Ho 1978: 42–3). About 70 per cent of the rural population were either tenants or very small part-owners (ibid.: 1978: 42–3). Their plots averaged less than one hectare and their rents were in excess of 50 per cent of the primary crops (Shen 1964: 41). Overall, the people of Taiwan suffered very poor economic conditions.

In 1905, the Japanese cemented their domination of Taiwan by deposing the large absentee landlords and making Taiwan's resident landlords responsible for collection of taxes on agricultural land (Hamilton 1983). Large portions of agricultural output were marketed and exported to Japan in order to pay these land taxes. These small landlords were effectively forced to act as intermediaries in the commercialization of Taiwan's agriculture. By the 1920s over 80 per cent of Taiwan's exports were food products. More strikingly, 50 per cent of the total output of rice in Taiwan was exported. This made up about 20 per cent of Taiwan's total exports and provided 30 per cent of Japan's import requirements for rice. Ninety per cent of Taiwan's total output of sugar was exported, constituting 50 per cent of its exports and providing about 75 per cent of Japan's total sugar consumption (Ho 1978: 30–1). Japan directed Taiwan's development efforts towards increasing the productivity of its land and simultaneously exporting its surplus.

Under this system, the resources, human efforts, and skill of Taiwan's people were not utilized to meet their needs, but instead were used to meet Japan's needs. The Taiwanese population's standard of living was neglected and depressed. During the 1930s, 75 per cent of the rice produced was sold in urban areas or was exported to Japan (ibid.: 68). Rice and other agricultural exports earned approximately 90 per cent of Taiwan's foreign exchange (Shen 1964: xxiv). Clearly these export earnings gave Taiwan the potential to substantially expand both its imports and its investment to meet its population's needs. However, the Japanese government's active involvement in Taiwan's development was explicitly directed towards capturing the exportable surplus and utilizing it to advance Japanese aims – not to improve Taiwanese living standards. Japan expanded and concentrated its economic power in the industrial, financial and commercial sectors (the sugar refineries, rice processing mills, banks and trading companies). Japan controlled the flow and utilization of surplus to these sectors. Thus, while output was rapidly increased, real wages and consumption were kept very low (Ho 1978: 32). The pattern of development imposed by the Japanese benefitted Japan, but was very oppressive to the Taiwanese.

The Japanese colonial state in Korea established a new agrarian structure very similar to that operating in Taiwan. Ownership rights were transformed in conjunction with a major land survey from 1910 to 1918. As much as 50 per cent of agriculture and forest lands were concentrated in the hands of Japanese government and corporate agencies. Much of the rest was held by Korean landlords who cooperated with Japanese policies. By the late 1930s, more than 2/3 of the cultivated land area was concentrated in the hands of only 3 per cent of landowners (Amsden 1989: 54). Japanese policies encouraged investment in agriculture and implementation of modern techniques led to a substantial increase in agricultural output – 38 per cent from 1912 to 1936. They also encouraged a much more dramatic increase in exports, over 700 per cent during the same period, so that by 1936 Korea was exporting more than half of its production of rice (Hart-Landsberg 1993: 105). Not surprisingly, during this period more peasants were forced in to tenancy (from 38 per cent of households to 54 per cent (Amsden 1989: 54) overall, with closer to 90 per cent in the south (Hart-Landsberg 1993: 105)), rents rose to over 80 per cent of output in the south (ibid.: 105) and material living conditions of the peasantry declined. Their consumption of basic food stuffs decreased by almost 40 per cent during the period of output and export growth (Amsden 1989: 54).

Taiwan's land reform

Taiwan's postwar land reform was specifically designed to address widespread landlessness, ultra-small holdings, poor living conditions and poor expectations for the future (Shen 1964: 41). The government believed that sweeping land reforms would stabilize the rural social order and raise morale for a fight against communist incursion from the mainland (Shen 1970: 57). The first, de facto, phase of land reform in Taiwan was the confiscation of 'enemy' property. In Taiwan, all Japanese properties were seized, which amounted to 20 per cent of the total arable land (Ho 1978: 161). The second phase involved the imposition of rent reductions. In Taiwan, tenure on tenant land was secured and rents were strictly limited to a maximum of 37.5 per cent of the major crop (reduced in some cases from 70 per cent) (Shen 1970: 57). The reductions instigated distress sales of landlord property. As a result, peasants took ownership of 5 per cent of Taiwan's total arable land at low prices (ibid.: 59). The sale of public land followed rent reductions. The Taiwan government kept control of the large former Japanese sugar estates through TaiSugar (approximately 10 per cent of the total arable land), but sold other confiscated land to former tenants on relatively easy terms. Over a ten-year period an additional 10 per cent of Taiwan's arable land was sold (under ten-year mortgages payable in rice or sweet potatoes) to peasants in this program (ibid.: 60).

The 'Land-to-the-Tiller' phase of Taiwan's land reform expropriated an additional 16 per cent of total arable lands (and 25 per cent of all paddy) (Shen 1964: 44). Lands in excess of 3 ha. for paddy or

6 ha. dry land (medium-grade) that were previously leased or worked by laborers were subject to compulsory sale. Landlords in Taiwan were compensated with ten-year crop (rice or sweet potato) denominated bonds at 4 per cent interest (which made up 70 per cent of total compensation) and with shares in government-owned industries (30 per cent). Peasants paid this same price, in crop at four per cent interest, also over a ten-year period (Shen 1970: 61–4).

The effects of land reform in Taiwan were dramatic. The proportion of peasants who were landowners rose from 30 per cent to 77 per cent; the proportion who were strictly tenants fell from 40 per cent to 11 per cent (Ho 1978: 335). The reduction of landless peasants from 40 per cent to 17 per cent helped to reduce acute rural unemployment (Ho 1978: 144; Koo 1968: 35). During the first five years after land reform, consumption, public and private investment, and output in the agricultural sector all rose significantly (Shen 1970: 65). Most of the income increase went to the small farmers (Ho 1978: 168–70). In sum, close to 60 per cent of Taiwan's farm households benefitted from the land reform (Shen 1964: 70). Land reform helped to maintain relatively egalitarian income distribution (Ho 1978: 144) while it provided a foundation for industrial development.

South Korea's land reform

At the end of World War II, approximately 50 per cent of Korean peasants were tenants, 35 per cent were part-owner and part-tenant and 14 per cent were owner-operators (Morrow and Sherper 1970: 17). The United States occupation government undertook to distribute former Japanese holdings – about 14 per cent of the total farmland – to the tenants. Another phase of land reform was carried out by the Korean government at the end of the occupation period. The Land Reform Act was passed in 1949 and the budget for implementation was passed the next year. Sixteen per cent of farmland changed hands under this program, which distributed land held in tracts of three hectares or more.

Two-thirds of farm families were affected directly by the reform, but the indirect effects of the reform were also important. Once the land reform law was passed and before implementation could begin, many of the landowners sold their land to small-holders on the private market (ibid.: ii). This turned out to be a very astute move on the part of landlords, since the government payments to land-lords were confiscatory. The government controlled the price of rice on which the payments were based. The government's late payments meant that rapid inflation decreased the value of the government bonds, denominated in rice, that were used in payment for the seized lands (Steele 1964; Ban, Moon and Perkins 1980: 287–8). The Korean government gained from this transaction, at least partly inadvertently, at the expense of the landlords, who had collaborated with the Japanese during their rule. These landlords no longer had political legitimacy among the population and they were therefore unable to redress their adverse political situation. The peasants, who paid for their land with rice over five years (at 125 per cent of its average annual yield), did not gain from the inflation but the land reform transformed village communities into more stable, productive and homogeneous groups.

Cooperative ventures and joint village activities were stimulated by the land reform (Tchah 1977: 22). Villagers relied on traditional social structures to develop their productive potentials. Village-supervised community development projects were stimulated by the existence of a surplus which did not go to Japanese or Korean land-lords. The major expansion of fully irrigated agricultural land took place between 1956 and 1960 as a result of these processes (Cole and Lyman 1971: 146). Output and living standards were further raised by these projects.

This period was followed up by a Korean government-organized drive to increase the cultivated area in the country. Planted area increased 20 per cent between 1959 and 1965 because of large-scale labor-intensive construction projects. Irrigated area was expanded and bench-terracing on the lower slopes of Korea's hillsides was increased. These projects were financed partly through the United States agricultural commodities donations. This program provided forty-five million days of employment when the drive was at its peak in 1965 (ibid.: 145–6).

Land reform, cooperative effort and agricultural output

Taiwan

The rural economies of Asian rice-producing countries such as China, Japan, Korea and Taiwan have historically been centered on the agricultural production of wet-rice in flooded fields. The technology of this type of production necessitates cooperation on the local level, and often on the provincial and state level, because construction, maintenance and administration of networks of irrigation and drainage facilities is necessary.

Taiwan's government helped to produce the conditions for the development of small-scale peasant agriculture. The rent reductions, land sales and land reform enacted by the government gave peasants access to land. The payment for land, land taxes, water fees, etc. in crop, at rates substantially lower than historical norms, helped peasants retain their land (Li 1988: 64). Farmers' associations and government extension programs provided peasants with modern techniques and inputs and with cooperative facilities for storage and processing (Li 1988: 64; Shen 1970: 185). The government provided irrigation and flood control facilities, new roads to markets, electricity and other important elements of an economic infrastructure. These inputs, services and infrastructure increased the productivity of peasant agriculture and lowered its costs. The government and cooperative institutions replaced exploitative moneylenders to provide credit that enabled peasants to dramatically increase their working capital (especially fertilizer, pesticides and feed) (Shen 1970: 207 and 65). Peasants could repay these loans with crop from their consequent increased output. Altogether, secure land ownership, increased inputs, services and infrastructure, and low-cost credit which could be repaid independently of price fluctuations, increased the stability and prosperity of peasant agriculture.

Taiwan's state policies not only created the conditions for the development and growth of peasant agriculture; they also created conditions under which a significant portion of the agricultural resources and agricultural surplus were transferred to the government. State-sponsored land reform effectively eliminated both the landlord class and large-scale, private agroexporters. For example, the expropriation of land and mills belonging to Japanese owners enabled the government to establish the Taiwan Sugar Corporation (Tai Sugar) (Shen 1964: 195). TaiSugar's exports constituted 50 to 80 per cent of Taiwan's total yearly export revenues during the 1950s (ibid.: 302). Revenues from rice exports, also controlled by the government, made up an additional 10 to 25 per cent of total exports during this period (ibid.: 302). Thus, the Taiwan state's extensive disruption and transformation of the pre-existing socioeconomic structure allowed it to establish and stabilize new (state and independent peasant) social relations of production in agriculture and simultaneously enabled the government to control and benefit from the bulk of agricultural exports and to subsidize industrial development (Ho 1978: 180–1).

Taiwan's rice-fertilizer barter program illustrates how its interventionist state was able to encourage its small, independent agricultural producers to increase output (and to allow them some increase in consumption) and still enable the state to appropriate and control a larger surplus. The Taiwan government held a monopoly on imported and (much more expensive) domestically produced fertilizer. The types of rice planted in Taiwan produced much greater yields when heavily fertilized. The government bartered its fertilizer in exchange for rice at high relative prices. The government was able to gain control over 25 to 30 per cent of Taiwan's annual rice production through rice-fertilizer barter (62 per cent of the government's total), tax collection in kind (13 per cent) and compulsory rice sales (11 per cent) (Shen 1964: 333). Thus, the government captured most of the rice surplus and effectively protected and subsidized the development of domestic chemical and fertilizer industries. Together, these collections of rice (along with land purchase payments in rice) pressured peasants to produce, and to give up, a food surplus. The government was then able to utilize its supply of rice to stabilize the market price of rice at a low level, keep down government budget deficits by providing rations to the military and other employees, and restrain inflation of basic goods prices and thus guarantee a minimum livelihood for both the urban and rural populace.

Korea

The government in South Korea controlled marketing, credit, inputs, adoption of new technologies and the pricing of staple agricultural goods, through its cooperative organizations. After World War II, farmers' associations continued their financial and services role in the countryside and, in 1949, they took over the distribution of fertilizer. In 1961, all service and marketing functions were again unified under the National Agricultural Cooperative Federation

(NACF) for reasons of administrative efficiency. In the 1960s, also, 20,000 small cooperatives at the village level were merged into 1,500 larger cooperatives at the township level.

By the early 1970s, Reed (1979) observed the operation of the following communal activities in Korean villages: an all-village mutual assistance credit union, funeral funds, mutual assistance funds for social groups and cooperative work teams for transplanting rice. In addition, there were informal labor exchanges for rice and dry-field farming, house building and digging wells. Cooperative work teams were a more highly structured working arrangement with record keeping about numbers of hours worked and exchanges were in the same type of work or in rice or money. The informal exchanges were roughly equivalent in amount of labor but they were not necessarily the same activity (ibid.: 139–40). The village assemblies in rural Korea, made up of the patriarchs from each family, met regularly to make decisions concerning the social and economic life of the community (ibid.: 139). By the late 1970s, 83 per cent of farm households were cooperative members and the large township-sized cooperatives had an average membership of 1,300 (Republic of Korea 1981: 7). The cooperative movement attained a level of two million member families and it has maintained this level of membership since then despite a declining population in Korean agriculture. Thus, a major focus of federal government control of, and support to, the rural sector has been through the NACF.

The other two sectors of rural coordination are the local village governments, mentioned above, and the agricultural extension service, which works through the Office of Rural Development of the Department of Agriculture. The extension service funnels knowledge about improved techniques through the other two groups. The very hierarchical aspects of the Korean government and the Cooperative Association are moderated by the election of officers of the township and village cooperatives and the leadership of village assemblies. It is reasonable to say that there has been a dualistic political structure in Korea – divided between local, more participatory forms of decision making and national institutions which have been very tightly controlled and carefully planned by undemocratic governments in South Korea throughout most of its history.

Agriculture has grown at an average annual rate of over 3 per cent per year since World War II. As the growth rate of GNP speeded up in the 1960s and 1970s, so did the agricultural growth rate, but agriculture's growth rates were always below those of other sectors. After the initial phases of growth of agricultural production which resulted largely from increases in the planted area, the Korean government, through the NACF, initiated a program of improvement in agricultural inputs and new seed varieties. The agricultural production function was changed through this program. As the demand for labor expanded in the service and industrial sectors, the use of mechanization, fertilizers, insecticides, herbicides and new varieties of seed, led to increased land and labor productivities in agriculture. Loans to the agricultural sector were used to pay for the fertilizer, pesticides and agricultural machinery that were provided by the NACF.

Agricultural investment has been self-financed by the agricultural sector, to a large extent. Between 40 and 70 per cent of agricultural loans have been financed from deposits from members of the agricultural cooperatives (ibid.: 10; Steinberg *et al.* 1984: c8). Although the Bank of Korea has provided most of the remaining resources, the Bank and the extension service and other government activities have been partly financed through the Korean government's pricing policy which, during the beginning of the industrialization process, kept the price of staples low in order to provide inexpensive inputs to the leading sectors in the Korean development plan. Thus, the agricultural sector has provided the cheap inputs necessary for development of investment funds for the agricultural sector and for the economy as a whole.

Improved labor productivity in agriculture provided the surplus labor and the surplus food for the development of the industrial and service sectors. Pricing policies of the NACF provided the foundation for agricultural development as input prices were not allowed to outrun output prices (Steinberg *et al.* 1984: 12–13). This kept incentives positive for the producers while allowing the government to pursue its primary goals of industrialization and development of the export sector.

US aid in Taiwan

Taiwan's integration into the international capitalist system is portrayed by many commentators as an unqualified success story that resulted from democracy and the free market. In practice, it was not so simple. Indeed, active, nondemocratic state intervention stabilized, developed and eventually linked Taiwan's economy to the international expansion of US capitalism.

The United States supported the defeat and the expropriation of the Japanese in Taiwan. Nationalization of industry and the banking system and control over foreign trade were directed against the Japanese and their allies. The expropriation of Japanese-held land and Taiwan's domestic land reform program broke Japan's influence and undermined its former allies' power in the countryside. Nationalization and land reform in Taiwan helped to dissolve Japanese economic and political institutions and power in the Far East while they stabilized the situation for the US. For example, as previously noted the expropriation of land and mills belonging to Japanese owners enabled Taiwan's government to establish the Taiwan Sugar Corporation (Shen 1964: 195) whose exports were the main source of revenue to pay for imports necessary for establishing a pro-US regime.

After the Korean War began, the US supported Taiwan as a check upon, and a counter-example to, the People's Republic of China. The Nationalist state was established on Taiwan by force; it was not democratically constituted. (It did not hold complete elections for its legislative branch until December 1991.) This lack of democracy did not deter US support since US objectives for Taiwan were to help it establish and maintain a strong defense establishment and a rapidly developing economy in order to demonstrate the superiority of 'free economic institutions' as instruments of social progress (Jacoby 1966: 137). Thus, for almost two decades the United States gave undemocratic Taiwan huge grants of military and economic aid in order to support its continued existence and development.

Steps taken in order to build a profitable export economy in Taiwan generated inequalities and conflicts. For example, the provision of adequate infrastructure and social services (education, public health, etc.) required considerable government expenditures. Poorly paid workers and firms struggling to be internationally competitive could not provide much tax revenue and government budget deficits would have risen without US aid. At the same time, without aid, economic development efforts would most likely have stimulated imports (including imports to the government sector) in excess of exports, creating a persistent trade gap and foreign exchange shortage (Fitzgerald 1986; Stallings 1986). Complicating matters, Taiwan's military budget was very large and created a potential conflict with the demands economic development placed on government revenues. The United States resolved these potential conflicts when it provided $2.7 billion in military aid, most of it between 1953 and 1962 (Ho 1978: 108–9). Per capita military aid per year from 1953 to 1957 was about $25, at a time when Taiwan's per capita GNP was less than $150.

Most US economic aid was given to Taiwan under the auspices of military support (Jacoby 1966: 42). Taiwan received almost $100 million a year in US economic aid from 1951 to 1965 (ibid.: 38). A total of approximately $14 billion (measured in 1987 prices) of economic and military grants and credits were contributed between 1945 and 1982 (see Appendix 1). The composition of the economic aid was 10 per cent consumption goods, 25 per cent capital goods and 60 per cent industrial materials (including grain, cotton fiber and fertilizer) (ibid.: 46). It provided food, clothing, means of production for building basic industries and, taken together, stabilized Taiwan's economy while it provided a basis for future economic growth.

The rapid agricultural development associated with land reform, which was the foundation for the distribution of economic benefits across social classes, would not have been achieved (at least not nearly as quickly) without US aid. Infrastructure and human services received 63 per cent of US aid (ibid.: 50) and 57 per cent of all capital assistance from the US (ibid.: 34). Agriculture received 20 per cent of all US aid. Aid provided 75 per cent of Taiwan's investment in infrastructure and 60 per cent of its investment in agriculture (ibid.: 51). The United States not only tolerated extensive state management of the economy and foreign trade; it also covered the costs of Taiwan's internal and external deficits. Domestic revenues, until the mid-1960s, rarely covered as much as 75 per cent of Taiwan's consolidated government spending. US aid financed most of these deficits (Ho 1978: 116).

US aid made extraordinary contributions to Taiwan's development. It kept military spending down, financed internal and external deficits, built up infrastructure, human services, agriculture and the public sector. Most importantly, the United States presided over (or grudgingly permitted) the dramatic social transformations and extensive state interventions that provided the foundation for rapid, materially beneficial development in Taiwan.

US aid in Korea

The United States provided development aid to South Korea from the late 1940s to the mid-1980s, but an assessment of the full extent of the impact of this aid on agriculture is difficult. In 1987 dollars, the total US grants and credits to South Korea from 1946–85 was over $26 billion (see Appendix 1 at the end of this volume). At times, the United States contributed as much as one-third of the Korean government budget. In the late 1950s, donations of grains from the United States (under PL 480) amounted to 9 per cent of the domestic crop.

When Food for Peace imports were no longer needed because of Korean self-sufficiency, wheat imports continued for use in the cities. To some extent, US wheat was competitive with domestic rice, but this was not a serious problem for farmers because their incomes were rising on account of the land reform and technical changes in the countryside which had increased output. The most important effects of US food donations to South Korea were in keeping the cost of food, and therefore wages, down. This helped industrial development considerably.

The AID Impact Evaluation report by Steinberg *et al.* (1984) suggests that specific projects, like the assistance in the construction of fertilizer plants, had a positive impact on Korean agricultural development, but that AID personnel had little influence on the policy level. This report found that the most fruitful focus of AID was its contributions to the cooperative organization, the NACF. 'Aid assisted in the construction of three fertilizer plants; provided technical assistance to NACF; and provided grants and loans for marketing, credit, mechanization, and grain storage' (ibid.: 7). The projects which accommodated the Korean schema of government planning, cooperatives and communal villages, worked very well. When AID recommended private distribution of fertilizers in the early 1960s, the government awarded a monopoly to the NACF instead (Powelson and Stock 1987: 184). The US experience with regard to the extension service and the spreading of technology through government help, on the other hand, fit very well into the Korean perspective on the proper role of government in development. AID sponsored advisors helped with the integration of agricultural guidance with agronomic research and research on mechanization (Steinberg *et al.* 1984: 15).

The $26 billion cost of keeping South Korea away from communism might seem excessive if the true amount of collectivism in Korean agriculture were recognized. Because of Cold War ideologies, aid advisors had every interest in minimizing the importance of Korean rural cooperation and portraying rural development as depending on the actions of small individual farmers. The reality was quite different and the importance of the Korean government plan, put into operation through the NACF and buttressed by large amounts of US aid, was unquestionable.

Conclusion

Isolated development by poor agroexport countries is improbable. Its alternative, international integration, tends to exacerbate budget and trade gaps. An extended period of social transition and economic expansion is necessary to reduce these gaps. Therefore long-term foreign assistance (aid, low-cost loans, privileged access to markets, etc.) similar to that proffered to Taiwan and South Korea by the United States is likely to be necessary to close these gaps and create the conditions for successful international integration and development.

Taiwan and South Korea's state policies not only produced the stability and equity conditions for the development and growth of peasant agriculture; they also transferred a significant portion of agricultural resources and agricultural surplus to the government. State-sponsored land reform effectively eliminated both the landlord class and large-scale, private agroexporters. Thus, in both cases, the state's extensive transformation of the pre-existing socioeconomic structure allowed it to establish and stabilize new (state and peasant) social relations of production in agriculture and simultaneously enabled the government to control and benefit from the bulk of agricultural exports in order to subsidize industrial development.

4
Industrialization in Taiwan and Korea

Introduction

In the postwar period, both Taiwan and South Korea were able to successfully integrate into the world capitalist economy while experiencing growth with equity (Li 1988: 53; and Amsden 1989: 38 (quoting the World Bank)). They both increased productivity and industrial output and achieved soaring exports, low debt levels, and stable prices alongside dramatically increasing real incomes (in Taiwan, for example, per capita consumption increased 400 per cent between 1952 and 1986 (Li 1988: 52)). In a view widely held among development agencies (USAID, World Bank, IMF) and analysts, primarily economists, Taiwan and South Korea's examples demonstrated the correct industrialization policies for all less-developed and former socialist nations. These agencies claimed that here were models that demonstrated the bright future of capitalist development throughout the less-developed world.

However, critics have pointed out that South Korea and Taiwan's success depended upon low wage, especially female, labor, imported technology and exports to increasingly contested developed country markets. Their development relied upon labor repression, environmental degradation and nondemocratic political regulation. Increasing competition from other low-wage developing countries in their traditional export industries, barriers to entry in high value-added, high-technology industries and intensified protection in their export markets make it difficult to reproduce the economic conditions of their success. Rising social movements in opposition to their labor, environmental and political policies challenge the political foundation of their model. Consequently, even before the East Asian financial crisis, critics contended that these two countries were poor models for developing countries to emulate (Bello and Rosenfeld 1990; Hart-Landsberg 1993).

Taiwan and South Korea's development was shaped both by US political and economic intervention and by Japanese economic intervention. US aid made considerable contributions to both South Korea and Taiwan's development. It kept their own military spending down, financed internal and external deficits, built up infrastructure, human services, agriculture and the public sector, and provided the materials, equipment and technology to build up the domestic industries that would later constitute their potent export sectors. Significantly, the United States presided over, or at least grudgingly accepted, the dramatic social transformations and extensive state interventions that provided the foundation for rapid, materially beneficial development in these two countries. Long-term foreign assistance (aid, low-cost loans, privileged access to markets, etc.) similar to that proffered to Taiwan and South Korea is necessary to close budget and trade gaps and create the space to develop the institutional and technological capacities for successful industrialization and development.

Taiwan and South Korea, in particular, benefitted from considerable US aid to their infrastructural development and capital formation. Both supported extensive land reforms and associated programs which secured the conditions for relatively prosperous, small family farms in agriculture. Each was able to carry out their own effective import-substituting industrialization programs while forging a strong state sector. They obtained substantial aid and advice, support in rooting out reactionary elites, transfers of technology, training, equipment and brokered access to, and information about, foreign markets as they became part of a US-dominated economic and political network. The development of their agricultural sectors, governmental capacities and a relatively diversified industrial base increased employment and incomes and improved the distribution of income and social services among much of the population. In other words, their successful development was predicated upon a certain connection with and, simultaneously, shaping of US interventions which sought to establish the conditions for capitalism in Northeast Asia.

Of particular interest is how Japanese agencies, particularly the *sogo shosha* (general trading companies), provided conditions for the successful production of exports in both countries and hence for their rapid growth. Taiwan and South Korean firms were simultaneously dependent on two factors: (i) Japanese firms' finance, designs, parts and materials, process technologies, distribution networks and marketing and (ii) state support to establish autonomous economic identities and to challenge their economic mentors. Taiwan and South Korea's successes, their future prospects and their relevance to other developing countries as models, are intricately tied into the institutionally and historically specific struggles with Japanese trading and other companies over the specific conditions of direct production, industrialization and export.

In other words, Taiwan and South Korea's development successes were 'institution-driven' more than market-driven because it was their particular ensemble of institutions and policies that enabled their successful participation in world markets and their integration into the world economy. We argue that it was this interrelated constellation of domestic policies, foreign intervention and aid and their particular integration into the growing and evolving North Pacific economy (bracketed in a relation with Japan and the US) that was the foundation for South Korea and Taiwan's economic success.

Aid and import-substituting industrialization

South Korea and Taiwan's successful industrializations, including their prodigious expansion of exports, were built upon carefully constructed, multilateral institutional foundations. Though they were built in response to external market messages and other economic and political stimuli, they were not spontaneous, rather, they were deeply grounded in specific institutions and policies. In general, the most important aspects of their industrializations were the development of the institutions and policies that enabled them to learn how to build and operate new industries, that provided them with assistance for these tasks and that integrated them into the existing structures of the US-dominated North Pacific political economy.

The United States helped set up and staff many of the agencies that planned and directed Taiwan's development. In this context, the US either allowed, or directly assisted, extensive development of the governmental and noncapitalist sectors, including government planning, government appropriation of the agricultural surplus, and import-substitution industrialization (Shen 1964: 39). During the 1950s Taiwan's imports exceeded its exports by 60 per cent and United States grant aid financed 90 per cent of the resulting trade deficit (Jacoby 1966: 98–9; Ho 1978: 115). In spite of the limitations placed on consumption and high real domestic interest rates, Taiwan's high levels of investment created a savings deficit. US aid financed nearly 40 per cent of Taiwan's gross domestic capital formation during the 1950s (Ho 1978: 115). Thus, Taiwan's internal and external deficits during its first 15 years of development were largely financed by US grant aid. Consequently, Taiwan was able to spend its revenues on development projects and to import necessary materials and equipment without incurring massive foreign debt or generating high domestic inflation.

Overall US economic aid to South Korea totaled about $6 billion (in current dollars) from 1946 to 1978 (Hart-Landsberg 1993: 145). 'The average annual inflow of aid from 1953 to 1958 was $270 million excluding military assistance, or roughly $12 per capita per year. This was nearly 15 per cent of the average annual gross national product (GNP) and over 80 per cent of foreign exchange (Cole and Lyman 1971)' (Amsden 1989: 39). Aid was oriented towards building up human and physical infrastructure, natural resource (including food) processing facilities and small-scale, labor-intensive consumption good industries (ibid.: 43).

Taiwan government agencies, in conjunction with USAID, gathered domestic resources, increased and improved the labor force, and obtained foreign technology, capital and imported inputs to establish basic, import-substituting industries in Taiwan. The first such industries were in (especially) textiles, food processing, garments, footwear, household goods and other simple, labor-intensive industries that could be relatively easily set up to supply domestic markets. The government provided protection through tariffs and quotas. The US supported these measures in order to provide basic consumer goods capacity to provide employment, income and consumer goods to gain domestic support and economic stability.

Firms in Korea – in sectors such as textiles, fertilizers, flour and construction – were allocated foreign currency so that they could import needed inputs, were given loans at subsidized rates and were granted tax exemptions. Aid financed imports of intermediate goods and raw materials targeted towards light industries (Amsden 1989: 45). Both light and heavy industry grew at rates of about 20 per cent per year from 1953 to 1958 (ibid.: 40). In particular, textiles, with tariff protection and subsidized credit, developed large-scale, modern plants for integrated spinning and weaving (ibid.: 41). A number of textile factories which had been founded by Japanese firms during the colonial period were later confiscated and turned over to Korean ownership (ibid.: 247). Cotton spinning and weaving in Korea received 10 per cent or more of total aid (ibid.: 65, quoting J.B. Kim 1966). In the 1950s and 1960s, cotton textiles accounted for over 20 per cent of manufacturing value-added while apparel counted for another 7 per cent (ibid.: 245). Textiles and garments subsequently became Korea's major export items (ibid.: 56).

Taiwan's textile industry provides an example of the connections between redistribution of assets, government assistance, foreign aid and industrialization. The Council on US Aid (CUSA), chaired by Taiwan's premier and composed of relevant cabinet ministers and advised by US agencies, directly promoted capitalist industrial development in cotton textiles. CUSA provided AID-financed raw cotton and capital equipment such as spindles and looms; loaned funds to provide working capital (in particular, they provided the local funds to meet payrolls); and guaranteed purchase of the output at profitable prices (Gold 1981: 70). The responsibility of the mills was limited to spinning and they gained valuable experience in an environment protected and directed by the government and its USAID advisors (ibid.: 10). The government favored small capitalists who had formerly operated textile mills on the mainland (in cities such as Shanghai). Among these were the founders of later textile giants such as Tai Yuan Textiles, Far Eastern Textiles and Chung Hsing Textiles. Although Taiwanese-born capitalists were involved in yarn spinning (e.g., Tainan Textiles), they specialized in weaving where the size and capital requirements (and hence, political pull) were less and the number of firms was much greater. Between 1951 and 1954 cotton yarn output increased 200 per cent while woollen yarn output increased by 400 per cent (Wade 1990: 79). After self-sufficiency was achieved in 1953, USAID and the Taiwan government began to encourage vertical integration of spinning and weaving to gain economies of scale.

This pattern was followed in other industries. '[T]he core of Taiwan's industrial establishment into the seventies had its origins in the protectionist period of the 1950s in labor-intensive industries...' (Gold 1981: 94). Textiles, plastics and electronics were the predominant cases. In the mid-1950s USAID, on the advice of a US consulting firm (JG White), helped to establish Formosa Plastics to manufacture polyvinyl chloride (PVC), the basic input for the manufacture of plastic goods. The plant was built under government supervision and handed over to Formosa Plastics to own and operate (Wade 1990: 80). Formosa Plastics diversified into rayon manufacture in 1964 and acrylics in 1967 as part of a joint venture with a Japanese firm (ibid.: 91). By the late 1970s, it became Taiwan's leading producer of manmade fibers (Gold 1981: 116). In the electronics industry in the early 1950s, USAID provided a Counterpart Fund loan which enabled Tatung to assemble watt hour meters with imported parts under license from Toshiba. Simultaneously, Taiwanese engineers were brought to Japan for the training (ibid.: 129) that enabled them to expand the number of electrical products that Tatung made domestically.

US aid and export-led industrialization

In 1958 USAID established its Office of Private Development. This signaled a shift from promotion of industrialization in order to meet basic needs and produce economic stability among the domestic population to support of private sector development and expanding exports. In Taiwan, as a condition for continuing aid, the US government pressured the adoption of a 19-point program of economic and financial reforms (Jacoby 1966: 134). It was intended to promote a business climate which would encourage private local and foreign investment, reduce government controls and participation in trade and industry and promote increased exports. Its adoption was rewarded with additional US aid (ibid.: 134). 'AID ... tied the Taiwan economy to the American and to some extent Japanese economies for supplies of primary commodities (especially American grain and cotton), industrial raw materials, technology, markets, financing and advice' (Gold 1981: 190).

In 1960, South Korea had a per capita income of just over $80, which was less than the incomes of El Salvador, Nicaragua and Honduras at that time. Imports were about 13 per cent of GNP, while exports, mostly primary commodities, were only 3 per cent. The country's large trade deficit and, hence, its growth were sustained only because massive US aid financed 70 per cent of South Korea's imports between 1953 and 1962 (Hart-Landsberg 1993: 26). In the early 1960s, the US government began to pressure South Korea to increase exports and to find a new source of aid. Aid was reduced from $225 million in 1960 to $71 million in 1965. Unable to raise funds from alternate or commercial sources, South Korea was forced to begin reform negotiations in 1964. Park shifted policies from import-substituting industrialization (ISI) to export-led development, but he did not reduce the state's role in the economy. South Korea continued to receive the funds it needed to cover its deficits and meet its debt obligations and so maintain its growth because it was willing to reestablish relations with Japan and support US military activities in Vietnam (ibid.: 144).

Between 1965 and 1973, South Korea sent over 300,000 troops to fight in Vietnam. Over $185 million received in payment for these military services from the US was remitted by those forces back to South Korea (ibid.: 147). The US purchased almost $540 million in supplies, construction and service contracts from South Korean businesses from 1966 to 1972 (ibid.: 147). 'During the key transition years of 1966 to 1969, approximately 30% of South Korea's foreign exchange earnings came from Vietnam-related operations' (ibid.: 148).

Japanese aid and export-led industrialization

The US government, with US corporate support, permitted reestablishment of large bank–industry alliances in Japan and encouraged the shift of Japanese resources from state social services to state assistance for industry. US firms licensed technologies to Japanese firms and supported their access to Korean War markets and to US domestic markets. Subsequently, the regional expansion of this Japanese 'managed' capitalism model established conditions for capitalist development by promoting widespread industrialization and, simultaneously, improved living conditions in South Korea and Taiwan.

In the early 1960s, rapid industrial growth led to labor shortages and real wage increases in Japan. Real wages in Japan, in both the core and contracting sectors, tripled from the early 1950s to the early 1970s. Much of the competitiveness of Japanese light industry was based upon low-cost labor (Yoshino 1974: 367). Overseas investment and sourcing became the means by which Japanese firms maintained their trade competitiveness (Ozawa 1979: 9). The loss of abundant low-wage labor crippled the operation and profitability of Japan's many small and medium-sized labor-intensive industrial firms (ibid.: 10). Since the production of these firms made up a significant proportion of total industrial output and exports, their difficulties threatened Japan's entire economic structure. At the same time the large *sogo shosha*, which supplied the small firms with inputs and marketed their output, suffered. With Japanese government support, a few of the larger companies (e.g., Mitsubishi and Mitsui) began to aggressively pursue the establishment of overseas production networks.

The establishment of overseas production networks by Japan's private sector firms was assisted by Japanese government aid programs according to Ozawa:

> [T]he Japanese government officially treats private overseas investments as an integral part of Japan's overseas economic assistance ... in the 1950s, Japan's reparation program helped to pave the way for the advance of Japan's trade and private overseas investments into the Asian region. (Ozawa 1979: 33–4)

Finally:

> ... from 1954 to 1958, over $1 billion of grant reparations payments and other forms of economic cooperation worth about $700 million were negotiated, and the 1960s saw increasing flows of reparations and economic aid supplementing such payments from Japan ... Since both reparations and economic aid were tied to the purchase of Japanese industrial products, new markets were opened for exports. (Ozawa 1979: 77).

In this context the role of the *sogo shosha* was particularly important because they served as the link between the Japanese government assistance programs, Japanese overseas investment and subcontracting activities and US markets. Post-1960, Japanese *sogo shosha* were increasingly active organizers of overseas production. They marshalled their own and others' capital, secured additional financing, prepared detailed marketing studies and technical reports, assisted in equipping and operating direct production facilities, supplied inputs and made long-term commitments to buy and sell the output of the small direct producers that they fostered (Yamamura 1973: 186). Their primary role was to establish and coordinate linkages; to forge a network of firms so that all would function more profitably (Yoshino and Lifson 1986).

The dramatic increase of Japanese exports to the US in the late 1950s and early 1960s required the Japanese to make large investments in expanding their capacity and developing their expertise in marketing, shipping, warehousing and selling goods in the US. Japanese firms, particularly the *sogo shosha*, built up the physical and informational networks to handle massive volumes of trade with the US in many different markets (Ozawa 1979: 22). This infrastructure served as the foundation for the large efforts they were making to expand productive activity in the rest of Asia. The bulk of Japanese firms' investment in Taiwan and South Korea was in manufacturing, while in the US it was in commerce and services (ibid.: 22–4). In particular, Japan's small and medium-sized manufacturing firms concentrated their investments, approximately 60 per cent, in Taiwan and South Korea. Continuing wage increases and revaluation of the Yen reduced the attractiveness of sundry goods (footwear, toys, sporting goods, etc.) produced in Japan. The trading companies were instrumental in helping small and medium-sized Japanese firms relocate their production to Taiwan and South Korea and retain their share of the US market (Yoshino 1974: 370). Until the early 1970s the bulk of the investments were in textile and electrical appliances and machinery (Ozawa 1979: 27, 29).

How were these small firms able to manage their transition into international investors/producers? The *sogo shosha* were the first group of Japanese firms to make the overseas investments to set up global marketing networks. They played a vital role in setting up overseas manufacturing ventures for the small Japanese enterprises whose products they used to export. Trading companies have also been financiers for small firms. When labor costs rose in Japan, they provided all the necessary assistance to help these firms to move to Taiwan and then South Korea. Japanese foreign direct investment rose dramatically in the late 1960s as these firms built up distribution, marketing and sales contacts and capacities in the US and, simultaneously, established low-cost production centers in Taiwan and South Korea. Although these units also produced for domestic markets, they focused their efforts on exports, primarily to third countries, the most prominent of which was the US. About half the total Japanese investment in overseas production facilities was by small and medium-sized industrial firms (ibid.: 28); while more than 50 per cent of total investments in production facilities were located in Taiwan or South Korea (ibid.: 29). The *sogo shosha* played a vital role by helping small industrial firms with their overseas investment (ibid.: 31).

The *sogo shosha* initially chose local partners in Taiwan and South Korea from among their own former distributors or independent local producers, that is, from among potential competitors (ibid.: 31). Mitsubishi led a group of trading companies to invest in small local firms to produce for South Korea's domestic market and, later, to export. In the vast majority of cases the trading companies imported parts and technology from associated companies in Japan and distributed South Korean output through their existing trade channels to Japan and the US. Mitsubishi sent a large delegation to Taiwan in 1965 to lay the groundwork for partnerships among the small Japanese firms it represented and local Taiwanese firms in a number of industries (e.g., chemical fibers, pharmaceuticals, farm machines). Subsequently, they provided the bulk of financing, technical support, means and market outlets for these ventures (Halliday and McCormack 1973: 136–8).

Impact of Japanese aid in South Korea

The contradictory character of South Korea's economic situation is best perceived from the often sharply contrasting views of those who study it. For example, in her influential book *Asia's Next Giant* Alice Amsden argues that, although South Korea follows Japan's path as a 'late industrializer' and perforce must learn from Japan, the distinctive character of Korean development is found in its state-led national capitalism (1989: 76–7). In her view the state sub-sidized, disciplined (with performance standards) and protected its domestic business groups so that they grew up to successfully compete in the international economy. In seeming contrast, Bruce Cumings (1984) has argued that there is an 'essential Japanese context' to Korean development and that in order to understand the regime's 'economic dynamism' one must begin with its location within a larger structure of US political and Japanese economic influence. These two aspects, despite their seeming contradiction, must be fused in order to produce a complete story of Korean development.

The integration of South Korea into the North Pacific political economy, the growth surge of its national firms and the increased direct participation of Japanese firms in these processes were initiated by the confluence of forces that produced normalization of relations with Japan in 1965. US security interests, Japanese economic interests and internal Korean political and economic circumstances combined to reintroduce direct Japanese participation into the Korean economy (Halliday and McCormack 1973: 148). Shortly after normalization, Japan and South Korea published a report which detailed plans for 'an international vertical division of labor' in which Japanese firms would subcontract out their labor-intensive export processing production to new industries in South Korea (McCormack 1978: 177). After the ratification of the Normalization Treaty, the Japan Economic Research Council and Korean Productivity Organization published a joint report which called for an expansion of export-processing activities in which Japanese materials and equipment were imported duty-free to be used by low-wage Korean labor to produce exports. Over 20 per cent of Korea's exports were produced in such conditions by 1969 (Hart-Landsberg 1993: 151). 'As part of the 1965 Japan–ROK Normalization Treaty, Japan agreed to give South Korea $200 million in public loans, $300 million in grants, and at least $300 million in commercial credits, to be paid over a ten year period beginning in 1966' (ibid.: 145). Japanese firms became dominant in cement, textiles, fertilizer, fibers, chemicals and machine building in South Korea (Halliday and McCormack 1973: 153) and South Korean direct producers were effectively integrated into the economic networks – the *keiretsu* (Yoshino 1974: 370) of the trading companies and their associated banks. Beginning in the 1960s Japanese firms helped Korean firms with new machinery and inputs of synthetic fibers and blends and enabled access to US markets (Amsden 1989: 248). From 1965 to 1982 Japan provided over $4 billion in public and commercial loans to Korea (Hart-Landsberg 1993: 148).

Japanese participation was usually in the form of technical licensing and subcontracting by both core firms and their suppliers. Short-term independent consultants from Japan played extremely influential roles in effectively transferring and implementing technology in Korean factories (Amsden 1989: 234). With the re-establishment of relations with South Korea, Japanese firms rapidly increased their investments in, and sourcing from, Korea, especially its Masan Free Export Processing Zone (MAFEZ) (Ozawa 1979: 15). Japanese firms were the dominant investors in MAFEZ (ibid.: 89). Japanese investors, usually small and medium firms, often took local partners and sourced their parts from traditional suppliers in Japan. Korean textile output grew at average annual rates in excess of 20 per cent during the 1970s (Amsden 1989: 253).

Impact of Japanese aid in Taiwan

In Taiwan, the agreements with Japan were less formal than those in the Korean case, and were primarily at the firm level. Some of the Taiwanese owners of small mills under the Japanese occupation became important textile capitalists during the 1950s; thus, they were in a position to become exporters during the 1960s. In 1948, Shanghai textile mill owners began shipping their equipment from the mainland to Taiwan (Gold 1981: 99). Many of the Shanghai textile firms had historical relations with the prewar Japanese *sogo shosha* (Yoshino 1974: 359). The first export industries were those developed during the period of import substitution. Textiles, garments and processed foods industries had the most experience and capacity. Of the top ten textile firms, all but one was founded before 1960 and that exception was an outgrowth of an earlier firm (Gold 1981: 110). Since the 1950s, Taiwan's electronics firms have licensed Japanese technology to develop new products and to solve production problems (ibid.: 134).

US firms began to relocate direct production of labor-intensive products to Taiwan and South Korea in order to compete with low-cost Japanese goods flooding US markets (Yoshino 1974: 367). In 1964, General Instruments became the first US electronics firm to come to Taiwan to use its low-cost labor to compete with the Japanese. Their transfer of production facilities was promoted as a model for US investment in Taiwan by USAID (Gold 1981: 196). General Instruments was quickly followed by Sylvania-Philco (1966), RCA (1967), Admiral (1967), Motorola (1969) and Zenith (1970). As a result of such developments, consumer electronics accounted for almost 75 per cent of Taiwan's electronics exports in the 1970s (ibid.: 198). The US firms manufactured almost completely for the US market. However, by the late 1970s almost 60 per cent of their materials, by value, were sourced in Taiwan (ibid.: 199). In 1963, Singer Sewing Machines set up a plant in Taiwan. It sourced the vast majority of its parts locally, transferred technology to its suppliers and increased exports from Taiwan (Gold 1986: 85).

Textile exports grew at rates close to 40 per cent a year until 1958 when Taiwan became a net exporter. Exports of textiles, post 1958, grew at a rate in excess of 40 per cent a year, with most of the output going to US markets (Wade 1993: 79). Exports of textiles as a percentage of total output rose from 20 per cent in 1961 to 80 per cent in 1972 (Gold 1986: 82). Garments were produced for foreign brands. In order to reach primarily US markets, Taiwanese firms sought assistance from, or they were sought out by, US mass market firms (e.g., Kmart, J.C. Penney, Woolworth and Sears among retailers (Ozawa 1979: 114); Arrow and Jantzen among name brand items). They manufactured goods for, among others, Arrow, Kmart or Munsingwear according to these mass marketers' designs and quality specifications. The US firms then marketed the output in the US (Gold 1981: 109).

In response to the early successes and in order to accelerate these trends the Taiwan government established the Kaoshiung Export Processing Zone (KEPZ) in 1966. The KEPZ provided a modern harbor and industrial park with modern infrastructure. Japanese investors (particularly small and medium firms) were the largest foreign investors in the KEPZ (Ozawa 1979: 87). Japanese firms in the KEPZ came there to lower costs or to match their competitors who had come earlier. Many of their suppliers came, too. Some Japanese firms imported equipment and materials from Japan via Hong Kong and then reexported the output from their Taiwan operations via Hong Kong, in order to reduce their taxes (Gold 1981: 184).

In 1966, the Taiwan government supported the establishment of their country as an electronics industry center. In 1967 the Council for International Economic Cooperation and Development (formerly the CUSA) organized major exhibitions to introduce local manufacturers to foreign investors. Their goal was to build up a new parts and components manufacturing sector. A technical agreement with Westinghouse allowed Tatung to produce electric fans. In 1962, Japanese television and radio manufacturers began to make technical agreements with Taiwan assemblers. The founder of a major Taiwanese electric products firm Sampo, Ch'en Mao-Pang, started producing electrical parts in the 1950s under license from Japan. In 1964 he merged his activities into Sampo and began to produce electrical appliances, especially televisions and refrigerators with technical assistance and parts from Sharp and Sony. Later Sampo broke into international markets with its own brand name. By the early 1980s the US market accounted for 80 per cent of Sampo's export sales (ibid.: 140–2).

In 1962, Matsushita began to produce televisions, audio equipment and other home appliances with help from its parent company. It began to export these products in 1964. The firm had close business and technical ties in the 1970s with over 300 local suppliers and produced with high local content (ibid.: 139). The Japanese government extended large loans, provided research assistance and tax incentives to encourage Japanese firms to move their labor-intensive manufacturing offshore in the 1970s. By 1975 about one-third of Japanese firms' foreign investment capital had been provided by the Japanese government (Ozawa 1979: 37). Consequently, most of the major Taiwanese firms (Tatung, Matsushita (Taiwan), Sampo) have had Japanese partners or they have relied on Japanese-loaned capital and technology to develop their export business (Gold 1981: 127).

The multinational sector of Taiwan's economy (RCA, Zenith, Admiral) produced televisions primarily for export in the 1970s. These multinational corporations were large assemblers fed by thousands of small suppliers. Their sources were Taiwanese and foreign firms which operated on the basis of technical cooperation agreements with US and Japanese firms. For example, in the late 1970s two Tatung subsidiaries (one jointly owned with RCA) signed technical cooperation agreements with Mitsubishi and Toshiba, respectively, to manufacture color picture tubes (ibid.: 200). Electronics exports from Taiwan grew 70 per cent in 1966 and over 200 per cent in 1967. Exports continued to increase at a compound annual rate of close to 60 per cent into the early 1970s. By 1978, Taiwan had overtaken Japan as the number one color TV exporter to the US, and by 1984, electrical and electronics goods passed textiles to become Taiwan's leading export sector (Wade 1990: 92).

Aid and integration within the North Pacific economy

The *sogo shosha* used financial and technical ties to increase the vertical integration of operations in Taiwan within their global network (Simon 1992b: 133). By pressing their Taiwanese partners to source parts, components, raw materials and equipment, and to obtain finance, operations and access to markets through them, the trading companies were able to absorb the bulk of the value-added produced. In 1970, at least 50 per cent of Taiwan's total trade (imports and exports) passed through Japanese *sogo shosha* (Halliday and McCormack 1973: 140). In 1978, the *sogo shosha*, together with US firms, accounted for 65 per cent of Taiwan's dramatically expanding trade. This percentage remained steady in succeeding years, with about 80 per cent of the joint total going through the *sogo shosha* alone (Cho 1987: 62). Over half of South Korea's trade was then with the US and Japan, with most of the imports coming from Japan and most of the exports going to the US (Lim 1985). In the late 1970s over 30 per cent of South Korean total trade was handled by Japanese trading companies (McCormack 1978: 179) and South Korea became a major host for investments by the *sogo shoshas'* small Japanese industrial partners in textiles, electrical appliances, toys and sporting goods. Their output was then exported to third countries, primarily to the US.

According to Gold (1981: 109), *sogo shosha* were 'indispensable' to Taiwanese industry, both as importers of materials and equipment and as exporters of finished product. These trading companies were particularly involved in handling imports of materials and equipment, providing letters of credit and in exporting textile and garments, mainly to the US (ibid.: 188). When Taiwanese producers began to vertically integrate to produce their own synthetic fibers, Japanese producers established the joint ventures and technology licenses which made this possible (ibid.: 124). *Sogo shosha* also negotiated technical cooperation contracts in the electrical, wire and cable industries to help them to overcome problems with manufacturing quality – including in the design of products, the selection of raw materials, the purchase of machines and other equipment, and in the manufacture and inspection processes (ibid.: 189).

Acceptance of carefully negotiated technological transfers in conjunction with Japanese trading companies (and, to a lesser extent, US mass marketers and multinational corporations) transformed South Korea and Taiwan, into increasingly wealthy exporters to US markets. In both South Korea and Taiwan, an overall pattern of manufacturing growth with strong import substitution preceding export expansion existed in virtually all sectors (de Melo 1985, quoted in Wade 1990: 84). In the early 1960s, the US received about 15 per cent of South Korea's exports; by 1970 the figure had reached about 50 per cent of a much greater total (Hart-Landsberg 158). Japanese firms provided the inputs and technology to support direct production by Taiwanese firms in Taiwan. These products were then marketed to the US by the Japanese firms. Taiwan's exports rose from 20 per cent of its rapidly rising GNP in 1964 to 60 per cent in 1986 (Li 1988: 173). In 1982, fully 55 per cent of Taiwan's exports were through Japanese *sogo shosha* (Cho 1987: 62). Two-thirds of Taiwan's total trade during this period was with either the US or Japan (Cho 1987: 59). Taiwan ran a large trade surplus with the US. During the 1980s, 40 per cent of Taiwan's exports, mostly consumption goods, went to the US (Li 1988: 52). Simultaneously, Taiwan ran a large trade deficit with Japan, mostly in the parts and equipment category. Taiwan's level of employment dramatically increased and its overall income levels, income distribution and social welfare improved (ibid.: 52–3).

Aid and heavy industrialization

In 1970, a Japanese plan was developed to expand the Northeast Asian vertical division of labor by shifting Japan's 'pollution and space-intensive' heavy and chemical industries to South Korea and Taiwan (McCormack 1978: 177). In the early 1970s, the social costs of a number of heavy and chemical industries in Japan were considered too high. Japanese planners were determined to locate other sites for the development of these industries. South Korea and, secondarily, Taiwan were identified as premier sites for investment (Ozawa 1979: 18–19).

The governments of Japan and South Korea created a number of committees to coordinate their economic activities. It was at conferences arranged by these committees that specific projects that would receive funds were agreed upon. For example, at the third conference in 1969 the Japanese government agreed to help finance, design and build the Pohang Integrated Steel Works, including a $124 million grant-and-loan agreement. In 1970, an additional $160 million was offered to build additional heavy and chemical industry plants and several light manufacturing export industries (Hart-Landsberg 1993: 145). The *sogo shosha*, as agents for Japan's government and private firms, provided technical and management support for the development of steel, shipbuilding and chemical industries in Taiwan and South Korea (Cumings 1984: 33). For example, Mitsubishi (the largest *sogo shosha*) provided the financing and organized the transfer of a modern steel manufacturing plant to South Korea in 1970. These efforts were at the root of a steady transformation of the composition of industry in Taiwan and South Korea. In 1961, the chemical and machinery industries produced 24 per cent of manufacturing value-added in Taiwan; by 1974 they produced 50 per cent of a greatly expanded total. In South Korea, the comparable figures were 23 per cent and 39 per cent. State policies in both Taiwan and South Korea stressed the steady creation of forward and backward production linkages. The value of local equipment in the first stage of construction of the Pohang steel mill was 12.5 per cent of the total; by the fourth and final stage, it had risen to 35 per cent (D'Costa 1994: 63).

Aid and recent technological advance

During the 1970s the various oil crises, increased protectionism, recessions in the US and increased competition from other low-cost production sites threatened Taiwan and South Korea's export industries. In Taiwan a labor shortage and doubling of real wages between 1976 and 1980 created problems for Taiwan's exports (Gold 1981:

98). In 1972, an AD Little company study had suggested a planned response of selectively building up heavy and capital-intensive industries. The restructured economy would emphasize capital- and technology-intensive industries in order to position Taiwan in a new niche in the international division of labor. The capital-intensive industries that were identified in the study included steel and chemicals (Gold 1981: 100), while the technology-intensive industry emphasized was electronics (Gold 1981: 133).

In 1977, with the express purpose of increasing the state's role in the planning, development and operation of the economy, the Taiwan government created the Council for Economic Planning and Development (CEPD). The CEPD promulgated a new ten-year plan (1980–1989) which stressed the development of technology intensive industries, such as computers, telecommunications and robotics, and urged increased vertical integration of the electronics industry to capture more of the value added. In 1980 a science-based industrial park was opened. It provided supporting infrastructure, low-cost engineers, access to technical institutes and local universities for R&D support (Gold 1981: 103).

South Korea's trade deficits soared in the early 1980s. In order to compensate for this, they began to restructure their economy with renewed efforts to source from Japan and export to the US. In conjunction with these efforts, Korea received over $4 billion of new development aid credits from Japan (Hart-Landsberg 1993: 148). South Korea's exports rose from 29 per cent of GNP in 1980 to 37 per cent in 1987. In 1980 South Korea's trade with the US was roughly in balance. By 1987, it was running a surplus of almost $10 billion (ibid.: 155). The US share of Korea's exports rose from about 25 per cent in 1980 to about 40 per cent in 1986 (ibid.: 159). During the 1980s, South Korea depended on Japan for about half its machinery, almost 60 per cent of its parts and about half its licensed technology (ibid.: 155). More than half of Korea's trade between 1962 and 1979 was accounted for by the US and Japan, with Japan increasingly the supplier of imports and with the US the major destination of exports (Lim 1985: 84).

South Korea and Taiwan's continued industrial development depended on 'borrowing' (by importing) technology and making it cost-competitive through a combination of low wages, productive workers and selective, conditional government subsidies (Amsden and Hikino 1993: 246). In order to compete effectively with imports or to be able to export, Taiwan's state subsidized new industries as long as they continued to raise productivity and improve product quality (Amsden 1994: 627). Exports became the key to Taiwan's and South Korea's productive efficiency because, on the one hand, they provided the basis to realize economies of scale and, on the other, they imposed the discipline of the world market on costs and so compelled the most profitable use of inputs. In this context, imported technology was carefully employed with a closely disciplined domestic labor force to produce competitive unit labor costs (Amsden and Hikino 1993: 245 and 247). Paradoxically, '[t]he quicker a country learns and the closer it approaches the world technological frontier, the sooner it exhausts the opportunities to grow by borrowing' (ibid.: 259). Therefore, in the view of some critics, borrowing becomes a less viable strategy as Taiwan and South Korea approach the world technological frontier (Amsden 1992: 25).

Taiwan and South Korea developed successfully, not just because of political oppression and low wages, but because, in part, they created the conditions necessary to rapidly approach and then closely follow the technological leaders. 'Industrial success in developing countries depends essentially on how well individual firms manage the process of technological and managerial development' (Lall 1994: 648). With strong institutional support, South Korea and Taiwan's firms have been able to follow the moving technological frontier closely (Simon 1992b: 125). Taiwan and South Korea successfully absorbed foreign technology because the conditions necessary for innovation were effectively established (Simon 1992a: 110).

When US economic aid programs were terminated in the mid to late 1960s, Japanese *sogo shosha* took over as the major providers of finance and technology to Taiwan and South Korea. They were the source of almost 60 per cent of foreign technical licenses in South Korea (Amsden 1989: 232). Thousands of South Korean nationals were sent to Japan to study with Japanese firms and institutes, including many shop-floor workers (ibid.: 233). Japanese firms also provided consultants who played key roles in the management of technological innovation on the shop-floor and in offices. Textiles and plastics firms' products and operations were upgraded in both countries and integrated into the *sogo shoshas'* export networks (Wade 1990: 91).

Taiwanese firms are still purchasers of technology, but they are no longer entirely dependent on external sources for their product and process know-how. Taiwan has increased the technological sophistication of its manufactured products. For example, Taiwanese firms are a source of sophisticated components in high-tech sectors of various industries – especially electronic components and computers (Simon 1992a: 104, 109). In 1953, Tatung signed Taiwan's first postwar licensing agreement with a Japanese firm. They gained the information and training (funded by USAID) necessary to produce electric watt meters (in conjunction with the increased electrification of the Taiwan countryside) from local components (Wade 1990: 93). In the late 1950s, Tatung was among the Taiwanese firms who contracted to produce electrical appliances such as fans, radios and rice cookers. Tatung then became a major electronics producer as electrical and electronic products became Taiwan's leading exports by 1984.

Conclusion

Taiwanese and South Korean firms learned to follow closely US and Japanese firms into enhanced positions within the North Pacific political economy. Gaining mastery of transferred technologies requires skills, effort and investment by the receiving firm (Lall 1992: 166). Learning technology makes possible increased interactions with other firms and institutions. Therefore, learning technologies requires not only transformation of direct production but also creates the opportunity to learn how to organize and administer; handle and process information; establish networks of suppliers, consultants and contractors; plan, finance and account for business operations; develop and market products; and train staff. In other words, capitalist firms in Taiwan and South Korea developed capacities to retain greater portions of the value-added produced and distributed within the North Pacific political economy.

Overall, Taiwan and South Korea's industrialization and export drives have been enormously successful in the period since the mid-1960s. In Taiwan, the share of manufacturing in GDP rose rapidly – from 22 per cent in 1960 to 37 per cent in 1977 (Wade 1990: 88), and the share of heavy to light industry increased from 50 per cent in 1965 to 60 per cent in 1984 (ibid.: 45). In South Korea the share increased from about 40 per cent in 1965 to about 50 per cent in 1975 (ibid.: 88). In 1962 Taiwan was 21st and South Korea 40th on the list of exporters to the US. By 1986, Taiwan was 4th, just behind Germany, and South Korea was 5th, just ahead of Great Britain (ibid.: 37). Real earnings per year in manufacturing increased more than 15 per cent per year from 1960 to 1980 in Taiwan. Between 1953 and 1986, real GNP per capita increased at a rate of over 6 per cent a year (ibid.: 38). At current rates of growth, per capita income in Taiwan will match that of Great Britain and Italy shortly after the turn of the century. As a result, the conditions of life have been dramatically raised in Taiwan and South Korea in a little less than two generations.

Taiwan and South Korea's economic success is unquestionable. We have shown, however, that it cannot be attributed solely to a 'free-market miracle.' Instead, success was hard won by significant redistribution of resources (especially land), large amounts of grant aid, careful planning by independent, development-oriented government agencies and by integration into institutions which provided ready access to lucrative US markets. On the other hand, we have also shown that critics' contentions that Taiwan and South Korea's economic success were primarily dependent on low-wage labor and repression of workers are wrong. Both countries grew rapidly while real wages rose and political freedoms increased.

5
US Intervention in Vietnam

Introduction

After the victory of the anticolonial communist (Viet Minh) forces in 1954 and the achievement of a temporary military settlement with the French at Geneva, the US became increasingly involved in Vietnamese politics. The 17th Parallel, which had been designated in the Geneva agreement as a demilitarized zone, was turned into a border between the Viet Minh-controlled North and the South, where a US-supported government was headed by Ngo Dinh Diem. The specifics of the origin of the US involvement are well documented elsewhere, and we need only recall here that by 1954 the US was providing 80 per cent of the funding for the French war in Indochina, and that by January 1955, the US had become the direct paymaster of the South Vietnamese military (Porter 1975: 4).

To American officials, Ngo Dinh Diem seemed like a good nationalist candidate to fill the vacuum left by the withdrawal of French official administration from Saigon. After serving a term as a mandarin official under the French in Central Vietnam, Diem had resigned in protest against the French refusal to allow more Vietnamese participation in affairs of state. His anticolonialism was individualist, however, for he did not join any of the diverse political organizations formed in the 1930s and 1940s to fight colonialism. In the early 1950s Diem laid the political foundation of his later administration by travelling to the US and cultivating the support of Senator John F. Kennedy and Senator Mike Mansfield. Frances Fitzgerald (1972: 108–10) suggests that the extension of

Diem's influence was accomplished through the Roman Catholic hierarchy in the US – Diem was a devout Roman Catholic residing in a seminary during his stay in the US.

In contrast, Diem's political base in his own country was weak, and apart from the Roman Catholics, who were less than 10 per cent of the Vietnamese population, he had few people whom he could trust as new administrative personnel. His administrative structure in Saigon, therefore, looked very much like the French administration and at least one-third of his officials had been administrators under the French. In order to strengthen his political base, Diem made an alliance with large landowners by choosing as his vice president Nguyen Ngoc Tho one of the country's most influential landlords. In addition, he chose large landowners to fill positions such as the head of the Ministry of Land Reform. This alliance with landlords shows a further similarity with the previous French administration (ibid.: 109–11). In promoting the interests of the large landholders in Vietnam, Americans essentially replaced the French. This strategy dovetailed with US worldwide interests in the 1950s which were seen as fighting communism and extending capitalist markets in the underdeveloped world.

US influence on economic policies

In the 1930s Cochin China, an area with fewer than 5 million people in Vietnam's southern region, produced 1.5 million metric tons (MT) of rice a year for export. This was more than any other country exported in that era and it was as much as the major rice exporters of the world – China, the US and Thailand – exported in the immediate post-WWII period. Production of rice, and agriculture in general, had declined drastically over the 1940s and early 1950s. Because of its history, however, South Vietnam was judged by policy makers to have a tremendous potential for agricultural production and export. The government of the Republic of Vietnam, therefore, established mechanisms to increase agricultural production and facilitate exports in a way which would be consistent with its political support.

The American advisers' policy in the countryside was particularly important because Vietnam had previously been such a large rice-exporting country. Policies were geared toward ensuring the reestab-

lishment of substantial rice exports within the framework of a capitalist market system. In addition to the political changes explained
in Chapter 2, the history of reliance on rice exports constrained the
US advisers from their more usual policy recommendations in Asian
land reforms. In Japan, Taiwan and South Korea the US advised
liberal land reforms with small retention limits and large-scale redistribution to former tenants. This was seen as the best way to
promote stability and prevent revolution in the countryside in these
nations. By contrast, US policies in Vietnam were conservative and
strongly supportive of landlords' interest – at least until the last
years of the war when most landlords had already been dispossessed
in the countryside because of the policies of the National Liberation
Front. The land reforms in Taiwan, South Korea and Japan could
more easily be liberal because gaining control of rice for export was
not as important in these countries. Those countries produce round
rice, a variety with little demand in world markets. If the landlord
system were not reestablished in Vietnam, on the other hand, the
whole mechanism for exporting over one million metric tons of rice
a year set up by the French, would be wasted since it was the landlords' share which was typically channelled toward the world
market. Since the peasants had experienced a rapid population
increase on a limited land area since the 1930s, they were consum-
ing larger amounts of rice. Without production increases, or landlords, they would channel little to the world market voluntarily.

At the beginning of the Diem administration, in 1956, an economic survey mission of the United Nations found little industry in
South Vietnam and no heavy industry. Existing industry had lost
the foreign-resident market with the exit of the French from
Vietnam. The survey concluded that South Vietnam lacked the basis
for a major development of heavy industry, but there were important opportunities for the establishment and subsequent expansion
of a range of small and medium-sized manufacturing enterprises.
These enterprises should emphasize the processing of the country's
agricultural and forestry products (Economic Survey Mission 1956).

Although emphasizing the need for South Vietnamese diversification of agricultural production, the survey pointed out the
meager amount of rice exports in 1956, 200 million tons (MT), as
compared with prewar exports. They saw no problem with the population growth which had occurred in the countryside since the

1930s, because Vietnam was still underpopulated compared with other Asian countries. The UN even advised labor-saving mechanization of agriculture, considering the thinness of population in rural areas (ibid.: 1–2).

UN criticisms of the newly established Diem government included reference to the large military expenditures of the regime and the continued dependence on the US and France for over half the government's resources. The mission concluded that expenditures should have gone more in the direction of economic development and that increased self-sufficiency would have been a preferable policy.

As a result of the ending of the war with the French, total output grew during the first five years of the Republic of Vietnam. Because of Saigon government policies, however, gross national product (GNP) did not increase in real per capita terms, even in this period of recovery from the First Indochina War. With people returning to the countryside, rice production increased by 50 per cent but rice exports did not go above 350,000 MT a year and averaged only 200,000 MT. Light manufacturing production, such as textile, sugar, glass, pharmaceuticals, wood products, and soft drinks, increased slightly. Rice production increases and small increases in other products were not sufficient, however, for a rising GNP per capita because rates of domestic investment were very low (1958 – 3.4 per cent of the GNP; 1959 – 1.8 per cent; 1960 – 4.8 per cent). According to Frank C. Child, an American advisor from the Michigan State University Vietnam Advisory Group, investments would have to double for economic growth to be a reality in South Vietnam. Money was available from the US, but 'the real economic effort and hard economic decisions have not yet been made, economic progress waits upon the exercise of aggressive leadership by those persons responsible for economic policy' (Child 1962: 4–11).

Because of Diem's land policies (covered in the next section) and the disposition of foreign funds to the rich and middle classes, their incomes increased while incomes of the majority were stagnant or decreasing. There was a housing and real-estate boom confined mainly to the 'European' sections of Saigon and Western consumer durables, such as cars and refrigerators, were traded in a rising market while the general economy stagnated (ibid.: 64).

From the outset, the US economic support in Vietnam was strongly geared to providing support for the police and military. There was strong Viet Minh influence in the countryside since at least 60 per cent of the countryside had been held by the Viet Minh before the Geneva Accords (Prosterman 1969: 329). The Saigon government fought against this influence by force supported by US funding. During the period of 1955–9: 80 per cent of US budgetary subsidies went to pay military expenses (Porter 1975: 5).

Between 1955 and 1975, the $21 billion in US aid (at 1987 prices) which went to Vietnam was directed through the Commercial Import Program. This program played an important role in US policy in Vietnam and in the Vietnamese economy. Inflation had been a problem in other Asian countries which had received large amounts of US aid. In order to subsidize heavily the military budget of the Saigon government without causing inflation, dollar credits were provided to the government of South Vietnam for the purchase of commodities from American suppliers which were jointly agreed on by both governments. The Saigon government then sold the credits to local importers in return for Vietnamese piasters at the official rate of exchange. The piasters were then put in the Central Bank of Vietnam in a counterpart fund and these funds were used as needed by the South Vietnamese government in ways previously agreed upon by the two governments (ibid.: 6–7). The increasing expenses of military personnel did not increase prices in South Vietnam significantly because these personnel and others purchased American goods which were imported. Because of a disparity between the official rate of exchange and the real market value of the piaster, importers were able to acquire goods at prices very much below their value on the Saigon market. Large profits were made by those Vietnamese who were able to obtain licenses to import. Vietnamese license holders often sold these import licenses to Chinese traders who were more familiar with markets and business. The living standards of a middle class of Vietnamese and Chinese traders, therefore, rose substantially as a result of the structure of the Commercial Import Program (ibid.: 8–9).

Another effect of this program was to raise the level of consumption goods imported and to discourage the import of capital goods since imported capital goods would not offset inflationary pressures as consumer goods did. Because fighting inflation was the primary aim, goods agreed on for import were almost totally consumer goods (ibid.: 13). Economic development objectives were thus ignored because the policy was to favor price stability.

The impact of the 'invasion' by the US Agency for International Development in Vietnam, with its hundreds of personnel, was overwhelming. By the 1970s, the skyline of Saigon was dotted with the white stucco structures which were used as housing for American personnel. American 'counterparts' were to shadow Vietnamese personnel. But the counterparts to even medium-level Saigon government (GVN) officials lived in considerable luxury. Even secretaries in USAID offices could afford an affluent lifestyle on their American salaries. Their Vietnamese counterparts, meanwhile, often lived much more modestly. For example, Nan Wiegersma observed that the wife of the head of an agricultural statistics agency was a street vendor while his American counterpart and his spouse had an upscale lifestyle with servants and a driver.

Political power was in the hands of the Americans, who made all of the important decisions in this context of overwhelming American power and money. USAID offices were sheltered behind walls in the US Embassy compound. It is there that advisory policies were drawn up. These policies were then enacted as legislation in a small unprotected building in downtown Saigon, where the legislature met. This legislation was signed into law and executive orders were issued from the very large and very well protected Presidential Palace.

Nan Wiegersma's private conversations with Vietnamese and ethnic Chinese living in Saigon revealed disdain for many of the policies which the Americans favored. A more human-resource based development program with government-planned market advancement seemed more natural to some Vietnamese who worked for the Americans and carried out American decisions. Specific project errors reflected the ignorance and misunderstanding which arose from an alienating and inappropriate American decision making structure.

Diem's land reforms

Ordinance 2, issued by the Diem government in January 1955, was its first attempt to deal with the issue of land tenure. It provided for a maximum rent of 25 per cent of the crop, security of tenure, and release from rental obligations in case of crop failure. In order to enjoy these provisions, the tenant had to sign a contract acknowledging the land as belonging to the owner of record according to the Saigon regime and not to the operator, as in the anticolonialist (Viet Minh) reform (Race 1970: 3).

Ordinance 2 was viewed in many rural areas as simply a means of confirming the land titles of absentee landlords. Since no rents had been paid to absentee landlords in large areas of the countryside under the Viet Minh, the rent of 25 per cent was not a reduction from the traditional amount of 50 per cent but an increase from nothing (Scigliano 1964: 121–3)! Price Gittinger, US Land Reform advisor to the Diem government, assessed the situation as follows:

> As implementation began, an interesting paradox in landlord and tenant attitudes emerged. Much of Free Viet Nam either recently had been recovered from Communist control or Viet Minh Communist forces still retained paramount influence. In these areas, particularly those in South Viet Nam, landlords had sometimes not collected rent for as long as eight years. Now, landlords looked upon the contract program as a means to assure them a rental of at least 25 per cent of the crop. On the other hand, tenants in these areas resisted the program since they had been paying no rent at all. (Gittinger 1959: 4)

This tenancy law, or reverse land reform, was thought necessary because tenancy was 'essential to achieving a highly productive and modernized agricultural sector' (MacPhail and Vaughan 1968: 3). 'Land-to-the-Tiller' policies which would abolish most tenancies would not provide large amounts of rice for export because much of the rice would be consumed rather than sold for rent payments.

The true purpose of the ordinance dealing with rents was made obvious by its enforcement procedures. The government made sure to register more than 700,000 rent contracts initially affecting one-half of South Vietnam's tenant farmers, but after the initial three-year period when landlord rights were returned, there was essentially no further enforcement. Most of the three-year contracts – which were later extended to five-year contracts – were allowed to lapse (Montgomery 1967). Enforcement procedures imposed criminal penalties equally on tenant and landlord. Tenants who were pressed to pay more than the legal minimum would therefore not find it in their interest to take the landlord to court, even if they could afford to do so and most often they could not. The result of this policy was that the average rate for rentals was 34 per cent, well above the legal maximum of 25 per cent (MacPhail and Vaughan 1968: 4).

In the countryside, Ordinance 2 created considerable resistance. In part to quell some of this and also to satisfy his US land reform advisors, Diem embarked on a very limited land redistribution pro-gramme, Ordinance 57. This measure restricted landlords to 100 hectares of land plus 15 hectares of family worship property (284 acres in all). These areas were about thirty times the retention limits implemented in other US-advised land reforms in Asia. The land-lords were allowed to select the particular area which they wished to retain. Regulations also ultimately gave landlords eight years in which to prove that they had made transfers to others prior to, not after, the new law. One land reform adviser reported that transfers to relatives and strawmen were common and that years after the land redistribution, he had met men who openly admitted that they still owned 2000 acres (Prosterman 1969: 330).

If all the land that was expropriated had been redistributed, the land reform might have affected 10 per cent of the South Vietnamese peasantry. These peasants would have had to pay for the land, however. Tenants who happened to be farming the expro-priated land were eligible to receive land, and they were to pay for it in six installments. The government was to repay the landlord with a 10 per cent cash downpayment and twelve-year government bonds carrying a 3 per cent interest rate. Cultivators who had taken land assigned to them by the Viet Minh, and had not paid back-rent and land taxes for those years, were ineligible for this reform.

Land expropriation began in 1958 and by 1961, 422,000 hectares had been taken by the government, but only about 55 per cent had been redistributed to former tenants (Republic of Vietnam 1967: 83). The former French-owned lands, which were mostly a gift to the Diem government from the government of France, amounted to 230,000 hectares but very little (only about 10 per cent) of that was distributed. Organized resistance against the Diem regime became widespread in 1961 and at this time continued implementation of the program was halted. Henceforth, local and provincial officials retained rent from the undistributed land (Prosterman 1969: 330).

If the purpose of Ordinance 57 was to win friends for the Diem government in the countryside, the limited conception of the law and its lack of enforcement prevented it from having its desired effect. Only 115,000 tenant households – or about 7 per cent of tenants in the country – actually benefitted from the reform. The reform was arbitrary in that only tenants who happened to rent certain lands were affected at all and the poorest of the rural population – the agricultural laborers – could not receive any land.

Diem was in favor of preserving and extending communal land in the villages, but only as a source of revenue for local government, not for redistribution. He decided that rentals of communal land should be auctioned off to the highest bidder and that revenues should be retained for local expenses (Bredo *et al.* 1968: 43). Locally appointed officials never got the increases in communal land that Diem had wanted. Instead, they gained control of undistributed land that had been expropriated under Ordinance 57 and they also controlled former French land.

The Diem land reform programs ran into two major difficulties, according to Bernard Fall. These were that (i) the people most likely to be hurt by the reforms were in charge of applying them; and (ii) the reforms themselves had a limited and conservative outlook (Fall 1964: 309). Diem himself was from the Central Lowlands and he was not a big landowner, but much of his support came from professional people and officials from landowning families as well as from landlords themselves. Vice President Nguyen Ngoc Tho tried to protect the interest of the landowners, as did the Minister of Land Reform. Furthermore, Diem's party, the National Revolutionary Movement, was led by people from landowning families and the predominance of landowners in important positions was not solely in national offices; this tendency also extended down to the provincial and village level (Toan 1971).

The landlords and the war

The largest amount of military and police aid which the US put in the hands of Diem's government was used for political repression of Viet Minh sympathizers in the countryside and for the repression of the religious sects which did not support Diem, the Hoa Hao Buddhists and the Cao Dai. As the Buddhists turned to demonstrations in the streets of Saigon, and self-immolations by fire were televised around the world, the US government realized that there was now a significant lack of support for the Diem government. President Kennedy withdrew political support from Diem. This withdrawal resulted in a coup and a group of military officers took over the Saigon government. The succession of governments which followed represented large landlord interests even more directly than Diem had – but these new governments were also receptive to Buddhist, and particularly Hoa Hao, interests.

As the military situation deteriorated in the countryside, the US entered the war with massive military support of the Saigon government. The Vietnamese landlords were able to use the military support of the US continuously to reassert their position in the countryside. Landlords would ride in on government jeeps as the army reoccupied an area which had been held by the new resistance forces known as the National Liberation Front (Race 1970: 19). Where this was not possible, they sometimes made agreements with local military commanders to collect their rents on a commission basis. A third method was to have the rents collected by local officials:

> In Dinh Toung, Bac Lieu, Gia Dinh, and An Giang provinces, for example, local officials were observed performing the role of rent collector, following the troops as they advance into contested areas. In some cases they kept as much as 30 per cent of the proceeds in exchange for this service. One veteran regional observer estimates that 50 per cent of the government forces in the countryside, working out of fortified positions, were among other things 'tax' and 'rent' collectors. In at least one case, it was reported that the army itself engaged in the operation, with officers sharing the collections with enlisted men. (Montgomery 1967: 10).

These practices evidently started near the end of the the Diem period with a circular which asked each Chief of Province to help the landlords to collect rent (Toan 1971). The political reason for this policy was not only to maintain the support of the landlords for the government, but also this policy was geared to prevent the rice harvest from getting into the hands of the National Liberation Front.

The amount of rent that landlords could charge in 'insecure' areas depended on the political and military strength of the National Liberation Front in that area. Insecurity usually meant that Saigon government forces, local officials and the military could only appear in the village during the daytime. In insecure areas, the Front cadres put pressure on the landlords on rent reduction and rent payments were lowest in these areas. A USAID official described the situation: 'In Dinh Truong province, for example, landlords are not even able to collect the 25 per cent rents permitted by law ... because peasants were able to use VC (Viet Cong or NLF military) activity to keep rent collectors out' (Montgomery 1967: 10).

As the revolution in the countryside proceeded, the former landowners moved to the provincial capitals or to Saigon or France. Since many were no longer able to collect rents, they found other means of supporting themselves and many, if not most, maintained powerful positions. Besides business, there were other pursuits for former landlords – such as professions, civil services and the military. Many landowners who did not consider themselves good at business and who did not have the required education for professions or civil service became urban landlords. The most lucrative position to be in as an urban landlord was to rent to the Americans who were using office space and housing in increasingly large quantities in Saigon and in the provincial capitals.

Then the escalation of the war which culminated in the Tet offensive finally caused the US advisors to switch to a liberal land policy. The strength of the Front was suddenly realized by Americans and this finally made US advisors more willing to drop their strong alliance with Vietnamese absentee landlords. The US had at long last determined that the primary goal of winning the war against the communists was more important than preserving the large landownership pattern and exports of rice. Rice exports had averaged only 200,000 MT from 1958 to 1964. With US saturation bombing of the countryside starting in 1964, population in urban areas increased from about 25 per cent of the population to over 36 per cent of the population of South Vietnam by 1970. Rice imports were needed to feed this growing urban population and imports increased from zero in 1964 to 700,000 MT in 1967 and 1968 (Wiegersma 1988: 212).

The power of the large landholders was broken in the countryside as NLF power grew and only then did the US realize that their former policies were untenable. US policy makers then decided to combine a liberal land reform with technical aid in agricultural production and other aid services in projects called 'pacification programs.' Along with land reform, the distribution of new high-yielding rice varieties and mechanical water pumps for irrigation were supposed to win the 'hearts and minds' of the Vietnamese peasants.

In addition to these programs, ordinances were passed to try to stop the landlords from resuming control in the countryside when the armed forces reoccupied an area. In November 1968 a decree prohibited officials and soldiers in newly secured villages from reinstalling landlords or helping to collect rents (Prosterman 1969: 332). Early in 1969, there was a decree creating a rent freeze in newly 'pacified' areas. This freeze on occupancy and rent was for one year from the date when the area was secured by Saigon forces. There was to be no change in occupancy or rent for the farmers actually cultivating the land if they had been cultivating that land for at least one year. After the freeze and after signing a legal contract, the landlord could continue to charge rent. This measure was one way for the Saigon government to buy time for the settlement of confused tenure in anticipation of the 'Land-to-the-Tiller' law which was being drafted. In April 1969, the rent freeze was extended to the whole country in anticipation that landlords would try to change the status of land in order to not have it expropriated by the upcoming 'Land-to-the-Tiller' law.

Along with this decision to create a liberal land policy expropriating large landlords, US advisors decided to diverge at this point from the real-estate transaction type of land reform which had been carried out in Korea, Taiwan and Japan. The war had become so costly to the Americans that advisors calculated that if the new land policy would change the direction of peasant sentiments and help the US win the war, this would be well worth the Americans donating the money to the Saigon government to pay off the landlords. According to a decree issued in July 1969, all installment payments on land already distributed were discontinued (USAID 'Review of Land Tenure'). The US, in addition, financed the whole 'Land-to-the-Tiller' Program which included an automated titling process using aerial photography and computers to print out the titles.

The economic reasoning behind the change in US policy was explained by Roy Prosterman, an originator of the new policy, at a US Agency for International Development Land Reform Conference in 1970. He stated that the cost of supporting massive land reform in all underdeveloped countries aided by the USA would be $1 for every $7 then being spent in foreign aid. Compensation being paid to the landlords by the US was critical because if landlords were afraid they would not be paid for their land, they would be opposed to any policy land reform. He explained that support of land reform would cost the Americans only 5 per cent of what was then being spent in Vietnam and that the existing position of the US in Vietnam was caused by the Americans not being able to deal with land reform (Prosterman 1970).

'Land-to-the-Tiller'

The Saigon government's 'Land-to-the-Tiller' law was signed by the then President Nguyen Van Thieu in March 1970 and implementation was begun late in that year. The stated purpose of the law was to enable the tillers of the soil to receive all the benefits of their labor. The law specified that this purpose would be accomplished by providing the cultivators with ownership rights and putting a low retention limit on landlords (20 hectares). This law was the result of continued US concern with winning the war and questioning of the validity of continued support of the landlords. USAID contracted with Stanford Research Institute to do a comprehensive study of land reform in Vietnam. The Institute conducted two surveys of attitudes about land reform. They found, interestingly enough, that in the Southern region the peasants had an overwhelming desire to own land (MacPhail and Vaughan 1968: 2). The landlords, however, were overwhelmingly against selling land. The report, based on their surveys, recommended legal and administrative reforms and organizational changes which would further land reform efforts. Prosterman, the land reform advisor associated with this study, then wrote land reform legislation which was handed to President Thieu for enactment and implementation (US Department of State Telegram 1970).

President Thieu, who had initially been against a comprehensive land reform, came to support this issue very strongly (Ho 1971). The attitude of most government officials to this law, however, was very negative because it was so heavily sponsored by the Americans (US Department of State Telegram 1970: 1). These officials still held some hope of recovering some of their own or their family's land from the NLF or, alternatively they – or their families – currently held lands which stood to be confiscated in the reform. Since these officials ultimately had to enforce the law, their continued disagreement proved to be a serious problem in some areas. The law outlined a program with much wider distribution plans than had previously been legislated by the government. The retention limit for landlords cultivating their own land was 15 hectares plus five hectares of land cultivated for religious purposes. All land above the retention limits was to be distributed to tenant farmers.

The distribution of the land was free to each farm family. The maximum area for distribution was three hectares in the Southern Region, where plots were fairly large, and one hectare in the Central Lowlands, where double-cropping was frequent. The existing tenant tillers had the first priority on plots to be distributed. Second in line were parents and spouses or children of war dead; next were soldiers and civil servants who had abandoned cultivation because of the war. Last in order of priority were farm laborers and it is clear that these poorest of the rural population had little chance of receiving land. Approximately one million hectares of land were supposed to be distributed under this law. It was expected that the distribution would take at least three years and would affect over half of the 1.2 million families who rented land. By October 1970, over 700,000 hectares had been registered by landlords for exemption from expropriation – a rather high figure considering the low retention limit.

The final version of the land reform program was very similar in structure to land distribution programs carried out in Taiwan and South Korea with US assistance and also somewhat similar also to the Japanese reform. The retention limits were certainly much closer to those liberal New Deal-style reforms which the US had previously supported than to the early Diem reforms. The major difference, which favored the Vietnamese tenants, was the lack of tenant payments for the land since the US was willing to pay the landlords as a mechanism for bailing out of an expensive war.

The effectiveness of the 'Land-to-the-Tiller' Program (LTT) varied throughout the country. In An Giang and Chau Duc provinces, where the Saigon government's influence was strong because of an alliance with the Hoa Hao Buddhist sect, the land reforms ran into great difficulties. In most of the rest of Vietnam landlord collections had become sporadic, at best, because of NLF influence or control, and the reform was much more successful (Tien 1971). This reverse correlation between government control and effectiveness of the reform was caused by the fact that LTT essentially legitimized what the National Liberation Front had already accomplished in the countryside – a rural revolution which displaced the absentee landlords.

In areas where the landlords were still strong, they often found ways of getting around the reform. As previously stated, absentee landlord power in rural areas had been greatly reduced before the LTT law was passed. Resident landlord power was still strong, however, in some areas. Most of the village and provincial adminis-trators as well as the judges in areas with Saigon government influence were from the landlord or landlord allied classes (Callison 1972). Judges from the landlord class decided cases in the interest of their friends and relatives. They tended to use technicalities favoring the landlords rather than following the intent of the law (ibid.: 1).

There were also conceptual problems with the land reform which were at least as important as its lack of enforcement in many areas. People who could not cultivate their own plots suffered inequities as a result of the land reform. Soldiers, old and disabled people who lived off the returns from their land because they were not able to perform the cultivation themselves often lost their land under the new law. In fact, in some areas they were more likely to lose their land than were the larger landlords with more influence in the village, because of the differential enforcement already discussed.

In addition, there was an emphasis on Western-style ownership and titles in the program which the tenants did not always under-stand. One US advisor met a large number of former tenants who had titles but did not realize that they were owners of the land and that they did not have to pay rent (Keane 1971). These peasants were used to having their rights determined in the context of the political economy of the village through oral agreement. The pieces of paper issued from computers, based on aerial photography, and brought into the village by foreigners were often unintelligible to the peasant. They would only have meaning if they were explained and promoted by local officials and advisors and this often did not happen because many of the officials and advisors identified themselves with the interests of the landlords.

Whether liberal or conservative, US land reform policy never had the results expected by US advisors in Vietnam. In this respect the American experience followed closely the experience of the French in their rural policies. No matter what the specifics of the law or regulation, American and French 'reforms' would always be influenced by the pro-Western Vietnamese who were enforcing them. Reforms could always be turned, one way or another, to the advantage of this minority. Americans never seemed to learn the lesson that they could not impose democratic or progressive reforms on Vietnam. There were essentially two reasons for this result: (i) the private property and market institutions sponsored by the US in Vietnam were, by nature, inegalitarian; and (ii) no really progressive reform could be effectively imposed by outsiders.

Vietnamese egalitarian and cooperative institutions stood in opposition to private property and market institutions imposed by the French and later by the Americans. Vietnamese control of public works and planning had from ancient times been important to the maintenance of production and the increases in production necessary to match population growth. This was very different from the Western bias toward the use of anarchic forces of the market in directing economic life. When market institutions led to tremendous inequality and landlordism, piecemeal policies of reform always seemed too little and too late and never really appealed to the average Vietnamese peasant. These reforms were not understandable from the traditional egalitarian or cooperative frameworks.

The Vietnamese who had some understanding of Western land titles and Western 'fee simple' property rights were sure to benefit. Even when some Western advisors could get beyond their alliance with this elite and understand some of the grievances of the average peasant, the advisors were usually unable to change policy. American policies were either naive or ineffective and they were often contradictory. Ultimately, with the American retreat, no answer to these problems was arrived at and Americans referred to the 'quagmire' that they were never able to really understand.

Economic change with rural revolution

The appeal of the NLF program in the countryside was not confined to poor peasants and it was not limited to areas that the NLF controlled. The NLF anti-landlord policies influenced the whole countryside and the technological advances which were accomplished in the 1950s and 1960s were mostly as a consequence of NLF policies. The exit of absentee landlords from essentially all areas except for broadcast rice areas (An Giang and Chau Doe Provinces where the Hao Hoa were predominant) caused many economic changes in the villages in the 1960s. With rents greatly reduced or nonexistent because of NLF activity, peasants were able to afford expenditures on new technology such as motor pumps, fertilizers and new varieties of rice. Increased cooperation in canal building was also a result of decreased landlord power in many areas. These were general changes in the countryside and they were not confined only to areas where the NLF had direct influence. By the middle 1960s, there had been an alteration in power relationships in most of the countryside resulting from NLF activities.

Modern inputs were purchased with the increased funds which had ended up in the hands of the rural population largely because of decreased rental payments. USAID made available new varieties of rice and these were distributed throughout South Vietnam via the private market. Fertilizer had become popular in South Vietnam in the 1950s and use of this input was greatly expanded in the 1960s. Motor pumps had also become available through USAID and these were marketed throughout South Vietnam in the 1960s.

Despite these technological changes, military operations in general, and particularly saturation bombing, resulted in population shifts which were the largest determinant of changes in cultivated area and production in the 1960s. Part, though not all, of this change can be measured by looking at statistics before the air war, in 1964, and after the US bombing policy was well under way in 1970. For South Vietnam as a whole, the percentage of the population living in urban areas increased from 26 per cent in 1964 to 36 per cent in 1970. For the Mekong Delta, urban population tripled in this time period, increasing from 6 per cent in 1964 to 18 per cent in 1970 (Wiegersma 1988: 212). In most areas of Vietnam, cropped area decreased, in the Delta, however, the technological changes almost exactly offset cropped area decreases because of population shifts (ibid.: 213). Despite changes which increased land productivity, war-related population shifts decreased agricultural output per capita, especially in food crops. Vietnam became dependent on agricultural imports by the late 1960s. This, added to an already existing dependence on the US to furnish industrial consumer goods, resulted in complete reliance on America to bolster the economy.

Technological and organizational changes affected production through area under cultivation, such as a move from single- to double-cropping, and not through increases in yields. This seems surprising since the new high-yielding varieties of rice were widely used, reaching 25 per cent of the total use by 1970. Yields of rice per hectare for South Vietnam for a twelve-year period from 1959 to 1970 show no perceptible increase in yields (ibid.: 215). In order to understand why this is true and to understand the effects of technology more precisely, we must take a closer look at each of the technological innovations and organizational changes in the context of Vietnam.

Canal building was one of the services organized by the NLF at the village level in many areas and US advisors also sponsored some projects. In the South, between 1960 and 1964, double-cropping increased from 30,000 to 77,000 hectares, largely because of canal building (Sansom 1967: 152). The NLF irrigation projects were small, encompassing at the most one or two villages, while the few US projects attempted were on a larger scale (Kuong 1972). Canal building was a task usually handled at the village level in traditional Vietnam and still accomplished in a cooperative manner in the Central Lowlands. It is not surprising, therefore, that once the power and control of absentee landlords disappeared, and the remaining landlords were constrained by the NLF movement, canal building was renewed in the Delta, even where the NLF was not directly in control (Sansom 1967: 15). This organizational change increased production through increasing cultivated area, not yields per hectare, for each crop.

Water pumps were another change which increased cultivated area. More people acquiring water pumps farmed larger areas. In areas studied by Robert Sansom (1967: 173), adopters averaged 2.5 hectares as opposed to 1.2 hectares for those who did not

Table 5.1 Changes in cultivated area in rice for selected provinces, Upper and Lower Delta, 1964 and 1968

Area (ha.)	1964–5	1968
Upper Delta		
Dinh Tuong	84,000	120,000
Long An	83,600	90,000
Kien Haa	101,100	105,000
Vinh Binh	178,700	130,000
Lower Delta		
Bac Lieu	92,400	120,000
Ba Xuyen	175,200	197,000
Phong Dinh	116,200	90,000
An Xuyen	103,200	110,000
An Giang	179,000	165,000

Source: Republic of Vietnam, *Agricultural Statistics Yearbook, 1968* (Saigon: Agricultural Economics and Statistics Services, 1969)

acquire pumps. Sansom exaggerated the effect of the water pump in Vietnam by taking the experience of two villages in Dinh Tuong province, within twenty-five miles of Saigon, to be that of the whole of the Upper Delta. Although cultivated area, and therefore production, increased in Dinh Tuong, these increases were not typical of all of the provinces in the Upper Delta (see Table 5.1). In summing up his argument about the advantages of investments like the motor pump for the Vietnamese peasants, Sansom brought in as comparison a province in the Lower Delta to show the contrast of an area which did not have the motor pump (ibid.: 179). Table 5.1 shows that for the late 1960s increases in production in that very province, Bac Lieu, were in line with the Dinh Tuong increases. This was a heavily NLF area which utilized canal building. Traditional mechanisms for increasing cultivated area were much more effective than Sansom realized – production increased considerably in Bac Lieu in the years immediately following Sansom's study.

The use of new 'miracle' varieties of rice was introduced in Vietnam in 1967 and their use grew to between 30 and 40 per cent of the crop in 1972. Although the high-yielding varieties performed outstandingly under experimental conditions in the Philippines, yielding from six to eight MT per hectare, Vietnamese conditions are very different. Very good water control and very large quantities of fertilizer are needed for the new varieties to perform as they are supposed to do. Most Vietnamese farmers did not have the appropriate conditions for the new varieties and could not afford the appropriate inputs. Richer farmers in the villages who could afford these inputs benefitted from investments in the new varieties much more than poorer farmers. The introduction of new varieties thus tended to exacerbate the inequalities in rural Vietnam in areas of Saigon government control.

Village study materials about a Delta village analyzed the introduction of the new varieties. This showed that larger farmers used fertilizer with their new variety seeds. Similarly, a small farmer who had started to use the new varieties on his plot of 0.5 hectares could not afford fertilizer at the time of study, but forecast that with larger output that year, the next year he might afford fertilizer in addition. This village was an area where the growing season was long enough for two crops of the new faster growing varieties to be grown, doubling output in some parts (US Department of State Airgram 1971: 4). The greatest advantage in using the new varieties was in multiple-cropping and even the small producer might benefit if he could acquire the new seeds although he would not benefit as much as the richer farmer.

In the Mekong Delta of South Vietnam, both technical innovations and canal building were responsible for increased output through expansion of multiple-cropping. These two types of changes, however, affected income distribution in opposite ways. The traditional canal building tended to equalize incomes while the water pump and new varieties increased inequality. The larger farmers, who received increased income from using water pumps and new varieties, were often able to invest in further labor-saving technical innovations such as roto-tillers and tractors. Some also invested in motor boats for transportation and sewing machines for home production. Consumer goods such as radios and small generators for lights and even televisions were purchased by some villagers (ibid.: 5).

Since not only these innovations, but also the war, affected the supply of rice in Vietnam, there was no overall increased supply and no accompanying price decreases with these technological advances. In fact, because of shortages, rice prices were rising in the late 1960s. With these price conditions and decreased population in the rural areas, demand for labor remained high in most parts of the Delta despite the labor-saving technology being introduced. Wage laborers were able to increase their real wages in some areas, although not nearly as much as the richer farmers increased their incomes (Tien 1971).

The net effect of rural change in the 1960s, when both techno-logy and the elimination of rents are considered, was nevertheless income equalizing in most parts of the country. It is ironic that technological advances sponsored by the US were a lot more effect-ive, on a broad basis, because of the policies and influence of the NLF. US development strategies were not nearly so effective in parts of the country where the US was more successful in its support of existing hierarchies.

Conclusions: economic results of US intervention

In areas outside the Delta, and particularly in central Vietnam, cropped area and production decreased in Vietnam during the period of the air war. The value of agricultural production for the whole of Vietnam increased from 1964 to 1970 because of large increases in high-value foods such as livestock, fish, poultry and eggs. These products largely fed the increasing market for luxury foods in the cities. Per capita value of agricultural production decreased during this period, despite the rising production of these high-value protein foods. The greater part of the increased urban population as well as the rural population could not afford these luxury foods and had to depend on the staple, rice.

Despite the efforts of thousands of USAID people who were directed toward trying to make South Vietnam self-sufficient in agri-culture (particularly rice), Southern Vietnam increased its depend-ence on US-financed imported food. In 1964, food imports into South Vietnam were about 3 per cent of total food use for the country; by 1970, however, imported food made up nearly 15 per cent of total domestic food consumption (Daly *et al.* 1973: 1). The air war in the countryside produced a flood of people into urban areas. These people could not be fed by the agricultural production of the country. The bombing created a huge food and resource deficit problem in Vietnam which was only alleviated by increased imports. In addition to grain imports, large amounts of other agricultural and manufactured goods were imported into Vietnam by 1970. Cotton, textiles and tobacco were imported, as were large amounts of industrial consumer goods.

Industry in Vietnam did not fare better than agriculture in the 1960s. Although the consumer-goods importing business was booming, this was all based on US funding. Even the processing industries which grew during this period – sugar refining, cigarette production, soft drinks and alcoholic beverage production – depended for the most part on imports and not on domestic resources. These imports would not have existed without almost total US support, since this was a period of low exports from South Vietnam.

The countryside was hit hard by the war, but the cities prospered because of a continuing influx of US funds. The new land reform policy in 1969 led to more landlord money being spent on imported goods, since the US was paying landlords for land that, in many cases, they were not able to make rent collections from. The prosperity in the cities, however, was very unequally distributed. Peasant refugees from the countryside came in search of work and they often did not find it, while those with money for investment in commerce grew more prosperous.

The US failure in Vietnam was primarily a failure in the countryside, where peasants, through their support of the NLF, finally broke the power of the landlords who were supported by the US for so long. The 'Land-to-the-Tiller' Program and technical innovations supported by the US did not change the basic direction of the war. The land reform, as we have seen, was not enforced in some regions, and it did not benefit landless laborers. The technical changes introduced through the market led to progress in some areas of the countryside, but increased inequalities in incomes as well. The US failure to promote reduced inequality in the countryside ultimately led to failure in the cities also. Former landlords and officials turned to commerce and grew rich on commercial import activities, which were made possible by large amounts of US aid. The character of the Commercial Import Program ensured that almost all imports were consumer goods. Investment goods were seldom imported and a balanced manufacturing sector could not be established in the cities of South Vietnam.

Ultimately, after the US defeat and within five years of the integration of the country, the Vietnamese economy began to grow. Vietnam has averaged an above 5 per cent growth rate since 1980 (IMF 1998a). When the United States re-established aid donations to Vietnam in the 1990s under the Clinton presidency, the conditions of support were vastly different from those operating between 1954 and 1975. In the 1990s, US aid has supplemented the Vietnamese development agenda instead of supplanting it with a US agenda.

Note

1. Judges honored backdated papers establishing worship land and also papers ceding back cultivation rights to the landlords which the tenants had been deceived into signing. There were hundreds of examples of lack of enforcement and landlord fraud which were collected and documented by the US advisors who favored land reform. There was an investigating committee which was appointed to look into the false worship land problem in An Giang province. Out of 375 cases which were investigated, 374 seemed falsified (Archard 1971).

6
United States Aid to El Salvador and Nicaragua

Introduction

US policy makers learned several military lessons from their long and disastrous intervention in Vietnam, which they subsequently employed in their engagements in Central America. For example, US ground troops were not utilized in the Central American conflict as they had been in Vietnam. Nevertheless, political-economic policies that were used in Vietnam, like the 'Land-to-the-Tiller' Program initiated toward the end of the US Vietnam intervention, were continued in Central America in the 1980s. The right-wing ideological perspective of the Reagan and Bush administrations (1981–92) in fact moved aid policies in El Salvador and Nicaragua further to the right from the 1960s/1970s Central America and East Asia policies. Aid policy toward the Salvadoran government and the Nicaraguan Contras (encamped along Nicaraguan borders during their Sandinista period) continued to (i) serve the elite of the region, (ii) intrude into the details of development strategy with a neoliberal bias; and (iii) waste the resources placed under the control of weak governments.

USAID funding in the 1980s usually supported conservative political priorities, such as those of the right-wing Salvadoran party Allianza Republicana Nacional (ARENA). Political compromise was sometimes essential, however, and the Reagan administration had to endorse the Christian Democrat Napoleon Duarte in El Salvador, when he was chosen for leadership of a ruling junta in the early 1980s, and later, when he was elected to the presidency. Nevertheless, in their choices regarding which organizations and programs to fund and which policies to support, USAID helped in the development of right-wing causes. This policy undermined the governing ability of some middle-of-the-road politicians who were officially supported, such as Duarte in El Salvador and Chamorro in Nicaragua.

In Nicaragua, support for the Somoza regime had shifted to support of the Contra opposition during the period of Sandinista rule (1979–90). The US was strongly opposed to Sandinista political and social policy which attempted to construct a 'mixed' economy consisting partly of socialized production and partly of private enterprise production. Despite the US support of radical land reform in East Asia in an earlier period, the Sandinista's egalitarian land reform policies particularly bothered US policy makers in the 1980s.

With the election of the National Opposition Union (UNO) in 1990, the US again returned their support to the Nicaraguan government. In their choice of projects, however, they supported groups in the right-wing part of the anti-Sandinista alliance, and this assistance greatly aided these groups in their eventual electoral success in 1996. Despite being politically effective in their right-wing agenda, USAID programs impeded development efforts in El Salvador and Nicaragua in the 1980s and 1990s.

In El Salvador in the 1980s and Nicaragua in the 1990s, the Reagan/Bush administrations changed the overall model of development assistance. The new program supported nontraditional export promotion and the liberalization of trade. This endangered many industries developed under Duarte and the Sandinistas and also previous administrations' import-substitution programs. Other policies reduced government sectors and converted agricultural cooperatives into small private farms. These directions fit more comfortably with the right-wing ARENA in El Salvador and with Arnoldo Alemán in Nicaragua than with the officially supported Duarte and Chamorro policies (Rosa 1993: 64–74).

Support for Salvadoran land reform

Following thirty years of right-wing military rule in El Salvador, young radical military officers took power in a bloodless coup in October 1979 and announced the formation of a new society. Agrarian reform was to be the central plank in their radical program.

Right-wing military officers and members of the oligarchy quickly organized against these Young Turks. Under the Carter administration, the US supported the land reform idea but US officials were dubious about the rebels and concerned about the movements of left-wing peasant unions in the countryside. Support for a centrist Christian Democratic alternative developed over the next few months, mainly at the instigation of US policy makers. The Young Turks were forced to flee the country and the Christian Democratic Party took power in another junta in February 1980.

The Carter administration proposed a $50 million aid program to help finance reforms, which they hoped would support the development of a Salvadoran political center not connected to either the oligarchy or left-wing political groups (Armstrong and Shenk 1982: 138–40). There were two members of the centrist junta, Zamora and Dada, who wanted to bridge the gap with the left-wing peasant unions and insurgents operating in the countryside. Mario Zamora was assassinated and Hector Dada resigned in protest. Napoleon Duarte, a man with good international contacts and centrist credentials, was then chosen to replace Dada.

When Duarte assumed office, he brought along with him, as a precondition, an agreement with the army about the enactment of further reforms (ibid.: 142). There were supposed to be three phases to the agrarian reform. Phase One was designed to expropriate portions of estates of 500 hectares (ha.) and larger. The proprietors were allowed to keep 100 to 150 hectares. The rest of the land would pass to the control of cooperative agricultural associations made up of former laborers and employees of the haciendas. The Salvadoran Institute of Agrarian Transformation (ISTA) had the responsibility of forming these cooperatives. Around 15 per cent of El Salvador's arable land should have been affected by this law, and 376 estates were marked for expropriation, but this number was later reduced to 250 (Simon and Stephens 1981: 9–13).

Phase One was opposed by the oligarchy and left-wing political groups. In particular, the left opposed it because peasant organizations such as the Union of Rural Workers (UTC) and the Christian Federation of Salvadoran Peasants (FECCAS) were left out of the distribution by the army as it expropriated land in the countryside and turned it over to the government-supported Salvadoran Communal Union (UCS). A state of siege initiated simultaneously with the implementation of the reform on 6 March 1980 was also used as a cover for the army and the National Guard to attack leftist strong-holds and abduct and kill leaders of left-wing labor and peasant organizations (Armstrong and Shenk 1981: 145–7).

Most of the owners of the large estates nationalized under Phase One were absentee landlords so that they initially put up little resist-ance as 500 agricultural technicians and the army carried out the land reform on the first thirty estates. Immediately thereafter, however, problems developed. Many landowners moved assets such as machin-ery and livestock across the Guatemalan border. About a quarter of the country's farm machinery was thus removed and 30 per cent of the livestock was slaughtered (Simon and Stephens 1981: 10).

The cooperatives which were set up by ISTA also suffered from a lack of credit and lack of inputs, both of which had been promised but were not delivered in a timely manner. Cooperatives were organ-ized to include permanent laborers and employees of the hacienda and this process often left out temporary or seasonal workers. These workers remained the majority of peasants in the countryside and they were not given a role in the cooperatives. In many cases, the new cooperative management reflected the previously existing hier-archy — either because ISTA tried to keep the existing management workers in their former positions or because the permanent workers elected them to these positions. On the other hand, in the regions where there was a significant change in management, the local national guard (ORDEN) often condemned this and proceeded to assassinate the new managers. Three weeks after the start of Phase One, Jorge Villacorta, Undersecretary of the Ministry of Agriculture, resigned over the deaths of two presidents and five directors of new peasant management organizations (ibid.: 4).

Phase Two of the land reform was supposed to affect estates of between 150 and 500 hectares. These estates included 70 per cent of El Salvador's coffee crop. Following the political backlash which resulted when Phase One was carried out, the second stage was can-celed in May 1980. Phase Three was the Land-to-the-Tiller phase of the land reform. It was successfully launched under a separate decree in April 1980. This United States sponsored initiative was designed by the same advisor, Roy Prosterman, who developed the Vietnamese Land-to-the-Tiller program. Two-thirds of the rented land covered by this reform was farmed in small plots. This land reform included mostly the poorer land, located on hillsides and not desirable for export crops. Small renters of this land tended to earn most of their income from waged labor, and not from their small plot. This factor makes the circumstances for this reform very different from Asian land-to-the-tiller programs. There were both technical and political problems with this phase of the land reform. The major technical problem was that the reform disregarded the system of crop rotation used by many small renters. Farmers often did not rent the same plot for several years in succession because of soil depletion. Phase Three unfortunately froze the system of plot rotation and required peasants to remain on the same land for thirty years.

The technical concerns were not the worst problem with the land reform, however. The potential beneficiaries of the Land-to-the-Tiller decree were threatened with dispossession and violence by owners and right-wing political groups. There were numerous illegal evictions caused by the slow pace of enforcing the reforms. Once the land reform was announced, a large number of peasants were threatened with eviction, and about 18 per cent of them were actually evicted (Simon and Stephens 1981: 61). Worse still, death squads attacked land reform officials and peasant union officials who were promoting the reform and the violence sometimes extended to the farmers themselves. Although 115,000 peasant families were legally eligible for receiving land under the law, farmers learned quickly about the dangers of applying for land. Only about a quarter of them made applications for land and only a small fraction actually received land (ibid.: 20).

Land reform results and policy changes

The results of Phase Three were significant mostly in the insecurity of land tenure it promoted and the trouble caused for peasants trying to acquire land. Overall agricultural productivity benefits were not significant because of the small number of households actually receiving land and the insecurity of political conditions in the country. Only Phase One had a positive effect on agricultural production in El Salvador. A study of 22 cooperatives commissioned by USAID found that in the years immediately following the land reform there were significant productivity increases (Powelson and Stock 1987: 234–5).

Because of the war raging in the countryside, the benefits of land reform were not possible to measure nationally. Overall production and exports declined in the decade of the 1980s because of the continuing hostilities. Declining exports and a shift in politics in El Salvador and in the United States led to US and Salvadoran policy moves which undercut even the limited land reforms which were being carried out. In 1982, sugar, cotton and grain were exempted from land reform. Sugar and cotton were export crops and a justification for exemption was based on this fact. By adding grain exemption, a peasant subsistence crop, further 'Land-to-the-Tiller' efforts effectively came to a standstill.

When the Reagan administration and its officials took over USAID policy in El Salvador in 1981, they initially adhered to Carter programs which were supportive of Christian Democratic policies and favored land reform. Napoleon Duarte had just been inaugurated as president at the time and it was hoped that his stature would help the forces of moderation. The right-wing policies and perspective of the Reagan administration nevertheless ultimately helped to undercut reforms that were carried out under the Christian Democrats. Kenneth Ellis, AID Rural Development Officer and Clement Weber, working in San Salvador during the Reagan administration indicated in 1988 (Ellis 1988) that breaking up the cooperatives and giving the land to individual peasants was a good idea. The policy of Duarte's right-wing opposition, ARENA, also sought to break up the cooperatives. The rationale of the Salvadoran right wing and USAID officials was that low agricultural production in the countryside and low recorded profits for cooperatives meant that the previous reform efforts had failed. There were several reasons for the poor performance of cooperatives in that time period. The civil war in the countryside made production and transportation of agricultural goods difficult. Also, there were allegations that some cooperatives were selling goods through nonofficial channels and that these goods missed being counted in official production and profitability accounts.[1]

USAID officials seemed to have a bias against the workers managing their own cooperative enterprises. They were working toward dividing up the cooperatives for the following reasons: (i) they claimed that the former landowners were managers and that the land reform meant that farms lost managerial talent; (ii) United

States AID donated funds for professional managers, but many of those hired did not like dealing with cooperative committees and had quit their jobs; and (iii) they believed that the cooperative concept was suspect because it had allegedly been borrowed from Nicaragua. These suppositions by AID officials in El Salvador in the 1980s seemed to demonstrate more about the right-wing ideological views of the Reagan administration than an understanding of the history of cooperatives in El Salvador. The actual models for the initial Salvadoran cooperative movement had come from Israel and Peru in the 1960s. As explained above, Carter administration aid policy had supported the establishment of more cooperatives in 1980 but left-wing groups were excluded from the establishment of these cooperatives. The Reagan–Bush aid policy and ARENA challenges ultimately proved successful in undercutting Christian Democratic policy in the countryside. Cooperative processes broke down in many areas and land was effectively divided between cooperative members who then proceeded to demand titles from the government for the purpose of receiving agricultural credit in their own names. Therefore, the success of ARENA in the election of 1988 was not entirely surprising, given the lack of support from Washington for the centrist program throughout the country and the lack of participation by the left. There were numerous charges of corruption against Duarte's Christian Democratic Party which were believed by a large segment of the Salvadoran population who saw many Duarte supporters under indictment with corruption charges. The boycott of the elections by the left-wing political parties sealed the fate of the centrist forces.

The Central American peace process, led by Oscar Arias of Costa Rica in the late 1980s, finally started to ease the political, ideological and military standoff in El Salvador. A peace accord was signed in 1992. US and international financial institutions have financed a transition which has included land distributions to the former combatants and tenants. The peace accords specified a land reform program which reaffirmed a constitutional limit of 245 hectares of land and provided for purchase of ex-landlord and government land for 40,000 families. Approximately half of these were ex-combatants on both sides and the other 50 per cent were tenants in contested (FMLN) areas. About 20,000 of these land distributions took place in the next five years and the rest became mired in a slow and bureaucratic process. The necessary agricultural credit programs specified in the accords were also often not forthcoming (Wood 1986: 82–8). Following the peace process, political differences have continued to hamper economic development efforts.

Postwar El Salvador, like Nicaragua, remains a country which is politically bifurcated, poor, and dominated by structural adjustment policies of international agencies, the US and native right-wing political groups. It would seem that with the end of the Cold War, international aid programs could finance truly redistributive land reform and supportive social programs in El Salvador. Unfortunately, this kind of positive program has been slow in coming.[2] Old rivalries and conservative biases of the international financial institutions have prevented new leaders from developing workable redistributive programs. Social programs after the war were weak, at least partly because of the right wing politics of ARENA which did not want to reward the communists and their allies who had fought against the right-wing and centrist forces for so long. The land redistribution program developed by Salvadoran leaders with US assistance was therefore (probably purposefully) difficult to enforce (Boyce 1995: 212–13).

Despite these shortcomings, the 1990s have been a period of partial economic recovery, with El Salvador averaging 5.2 per cent in growth of GDP between 1990 and 1997 (IMF 1998a: 154). Another sign of change developed with the electoral strategy of the left which resulted in the gain of many mayorships by left parties and the hope for further national gains in the next election.

Nicaragua and the Sandinistas

Nicaragua's pre-Sandinista history was politically shaped by a United States intervention which established, bolstered and protected the Somoza family dictatorship as part of the Cold War strategy of the US. Another important factor in the development of this small country had been its lack of diversity in production and trade and its dependence on exports of primary products like coffee and cotton. Previous to the Sandinista revolution, the wealthiest 5 per cent of the landowners held 85 per cent of the farmland. About 40 per cent of the land was held by the Somoza family or other very large landowners with over 355 ha. each. Another 44 per cent of land was held by medium sized farmers with 36 to 355 ha. (Deere *et al.* 1985: 77). The remaining 15 per cent of farmland, which belonged to small owners, produced the bulk of the food for Nicaragua.

With the Sandinista revolution, the properties of the Somoza family and their close associates were appropriated (the Somozas had left the country). This 20 per cent of farmland was high quality land used for agroexport crops. Many of these properties were turned into state farms while others became cooperatives. Over the process of the next ten years other land transfers resulted from voluntary sales of property of about 5 per cent as landlords saw the 'handwriting on the wall' and sold their property and/or left the country. An additional expropriation of about 7 per cent of farmland was legislated with compensation to the owners. A total of somewhat over 30 per cent of farmland changed hands through these various methods. Other small farmers benefitted from a rent reduction and tenure security campaign which decreased rents by about 60 per cent. Titles were distributed for newly distributed land and for peasant land that had been held without title. The initial response to these tenure changes was positive and agricultural production, and in particular food production, increased until 1984. Thereafter, political and economic conditions deteriorated in Nicaragua and, therefore, agricultural production declined.

Many large and medium-sized landowners remained in production in Nicaragua rather than risk government expropriation of their land, and the Sandinista government oriented their policies in an attempt to accommodate these large owners. The political strategy followed by the Sandinistas in these years was to foster a multiclass alliance which was needed for the development of a mixed economy. They believed that there were economies of scale in the agroexport sector that would be sacrificed with the break-up of large landholdings. As a consequence of this strategy, 80 per cent of the production of major agroexports was left in the large-scale private sector (Reinhardt 1987: 95).

The Sandinista government was willing to subsidize the expanded production of large and medium agroexport capitalists. As long as holders used their land productively, their continued ownership was guaranteed. They were supplied with credit to cover all working capital needs at an interest rate which was lower than the rate of inflation. The cost of capital for these producers was thus negative in real terms. These producers were also guaranteed profitable minimum prices. They paid low tax rates and they were given access to, and special rates on, foreign exchange so that they could readily obtain imported inputs and consumption goods. These large producers were even granted special representation in governing and technical support bodies (Collins *et al.* 1985: 40).

Despite all of these benefits, the larger landowners fought against Sandinista leadership both passively and actively. The Sandinistas were always seen as a threat to landowners exclusive control over land, labor and other resources. They did not trust the new government and they undoubtedly feared for a future in which they might lose the power to control the scope and direction of social change. As a result, the agroexporters' production fell short of pre-revolutionary levels, particularly after 1984, when landlords began to postpone reinvestments and maintenance of their properties. Thus, the landlords absorbed scarce resources through subsidies, credits and foreign exchange but the payoff to the government for their attempts to appease the agroexporters was meager.

This failure of the mixed economy policy was partly the responsibility of the US. Reagan's election and the Republican Party platform commitment to overturn the Nicaraguan revolution provided the owners of land and other properties with a meaningful, externally supported, alternative which mobilized them to more actively oppose the Sandinista revolution's goals. Large landlords joined and supported anti-Sandinista organizations in the US and helped to fund those who were fighting on the borders of Nicaragua in their attempt to overthrow the Sandinistas.

The Contra

When the Somozas left the country in 1980, many men from their former National Guard troops crossed Nicaragua's northern border into Honduras. These disaffected Nicaraguans formed the basis of a fighting force which would challenge the Sandinistas for most of their eleven-year term of government. It was widely reported in the United States press, during the conflict, that the Contra were mainly from *campesino* backgrounds (Branigan 1987: 1, A28–A29). This point was later recognized by some in the Sandinista leadership in their analysis of the war, of their defeat by US counterinsurgency and of the election of Violeta Chamorro in 1990. For example, Bendaña (1991: 13–18) showed, with the aid of an interview study, that many middle-level peasants tended to identify not with the programs for the poor which were developed by the Sandinistas but rather with the Contra politics. The anticommunist ideology directed at the National Guard in their training programs in an earlier period was taken very seriously by these peasants. The former National Guardsmen, and the medium-sized and small farmers who joined them on the border, saw private ownership of their own individual farms as their ideal and they feared and disliked the thought of collectivization. They were fighting against the possibility of further communalization of property. These troops even showed a penchant for choosing cooperatives as targets for raids whenever possible because they saw their struggle in these anti-collective terms (Branigan 1987: A29).

The financing and support of these Contra came initially from Somosistas and later in part from the string of Nicaraguans who initially supported the Sandinistas, or political parties in alliance with the Sandinistas, but who later disagreed with their political-economic policies and left the country. No matter what the other reasons were for the opposition of each of the leaders who fled the country in the first few years, concern about the possibility of a threatening economic direction with confiscations menacing private enterprise was usually involved (Christian 1986: 314–15). The group who left and organized in the US and elsewhere in support of the Contra had political perspectives which varied from the social democracy of Eden Pastora, a former Sandinista who opened up a Southern front against the Sandinistas, to members of the Conservative and Liberal Parties.

The official US pullout of AID from Nicaragua was in February 1981. Aid was canceled for the official reason that arms shipments from the Soviet block were moving through Nicaragua on their way to the revolutionary FMLN in El Salvador. These shipments were presumably also making their way through Honduras, since Nicaragua does not share a border with El Salvador. There were news reports that US intelligence had determined that arms shipments had slowed or halted by March 1982 but despite the opposition of what remained of the Carter advisers in Nicaragua, US aid was terminated by Reagan and Bush for the rest of the Sandinista term of office.

Reports vary about the exact timing of when the CIA began its Contra support and supply mission but estimates generally point to soon after Reagan took power, during the last half of 1981. Arrangements were simultaneously made with the government of Argentina to train and provide military advise for the new Contra armies and with the government of Honduras to house them on their territories (ibid.: 232–5).

Meanwhile, the government of Nicaragua had to scramble to find alternative international lending to handle the foreign exchange shortfall resulting from the USAID pullout. They were initially able to make these arrangements through a loan from Libya and grants from Mexico (ibid.: 227). Although individual Western European countries continued to support Nicaragua with small aid contributions, the Thatcher government's UK representative to the ECC successfully lobbied against proposed large-scale ECC loans (Deighton *et al.* 1983: 11).

The next period of escalation in the US-supported/ Contra-fought war with Nicaragua received wide press coverage. The US established a trade embargo of Nicaragua and mined their harbors in 1984. When the US congress cut off CIA funding to the Contra, the Reagan and Bush administrations found sufficient funding through selling arms to Iran (the Iran-Contra affair). The expenses of mobilization for fighting the Contra war and the US trade embargo further aggravated a deteriorating economic situation in Nicaragua. The idealism and enthusiasm of the Sandinistas and their supporters waned under the weight of these increasing military and economic hardships. Inflation turned from rapidly rising prices to runaway price increases. People whose wages were set, in government and industry, could not possibly keep up with the price increases. Only people in commerce had a chance of income parity because they could adjust their prices on a daily basis.

Motivation for carrying out the important work of government or industry deteriorated as people found that they were earning only a pittance compared to what their expenses had become, because of rising prices. Government officials and workers often had to turn their attention to second jobs in the commercial sector in order to make ends meet. The monetized economy increasingly broke down as employers and the government started to make payments in kind because of lack of popular trust in an out-of-control currency.

Price inflation created turmoil in the countryside as well. Prices of inputs skyrocketed and farmers were concerned that they could not find buyers for their crops at high enough prices to pay input costs and support themselves. Meanwhile, cooperatives and individual farmers could not find credit. Those who had saved in order to provide for their own credit needs found their accounts frozen. Structural reforms were enacted in 1988 to attempt to cope with these economic problems. The best that even Sandinistas could say about the reforms at the time was that they were hard but necessary. Poor Nicaraguans were hurt the worst because they could not keep up with price increases of basic necessities. Meanwhile, the worst consequences of war were, of course, the mounting military casualties.

The Contadora peace process was led by Oscar Arias, the Social Democratic president of Costa Rica. The five Central American presidents met together over a period of years and hammered out a peace proposal which was finally agreed to and signed in 1989. Following this peace accord, the CIA financed the return to Nicaragua of some 100 Miami leaders of the Contra movement and their families in time for them to participate in the February 1990 elections (*Newsweek*, 21 October 1991: 47–8). As the war wound down in 1988 and finally ended in 1989, there was no sense of victory for the embattled Sandinistas. As with the Vietnamese in an earlier period, their economy had been wrecked by war. The political economic choices which remained to them were restricted and difficult.

National Opposition Union (UNO)

Despite the political and economic quagmire described above, the Sandinistas were surprised in 1990 when Violeta Chamorro won the presidential election against their candidate Daniel Ortega. Chamorro was able to put together a group of centrist and right-wing parties known as the National Opposition Union (UNO) to govern, even though the Sandinistas remained as the single largest political party in the National Assembly.

The political environment over the next several months was characterized by governmental instability and radical change. A difficult transition agreement was worked out by Minister of the President Antonio Lacayo and the Sandinista assembly members. This Transition Protocol required difficult negotiating to reach a complex accommodation between the sides (*Envio* 1991e: 3). The most troublesome issue involved conflicts concerning property rights. A middle-of-the-road formula was arrived at which would return some properties to former owners while many other rural and urban properties would be divided between capitalists, workers, demobilized contras and members of the armed forces.

This agreement gave the UNO government room to maneuver and to reorganize according to a neoliberal model. Meanwhile, the right-wing parties associated with UNO were dissatisfied with any accommodations with the Sandinistas and they immediately started to organize their strength for a fight against the more centrist group in UNO. Their first move was to attack the initial property agreements, calling the Sandinistas' lame duck attempts to legalize the property transfers which had occurred during their period in office (laws 85 and 86), a *piñata* or 'party prize' for the Sandinistas.

There was considerable publicity about some urban properties, mainly houses, of those who left Nicaragua in the 1980s that were redistributed to Sandinistas. Nevertheless, Sandinistas tried to make the case that rural properties were another matter. They were not totally successful and part of the reason why land reforms which had favored *campesinos* came to be looked on with some suspicion was the urban property exchanges and the effects of laws 85 and 86 which linked the two kinds of property changes closely together. It was, of course, in the interest of the right wing to link these two types of changes as a way of recovering rural properties held by peasant producers. As a result, urban and rural contested properties remained a problem issue throughout the six-year term of Violeta Chamorro (1990–6).

In many ways the United States helped to keep the property conflicts alive and USAID also helped right-wing Nicaraguans to gain political power *vis-à-vis* the centrists in UNO. In 1995, for example, the Helms–Gonzales amendment passed by the US Congress threatened to cut off US aid if confiscated properties of former Somoza supporters, who were now US citizens, were not returned. A conference arranged by the Carter Center for Democracy and the United Nations Development Programme attempted to resolve these conflicts. This conference recommended compensation for former owners and the issuance of land titles to current rural cultivators so that they could have access to credit to enable increased investment (Mendoza 1995: 7–9).

AID and UNO

The United States had provided substantial financing for the Contra War, spending more than half a billion dollars a year in the mid and late 1980s. This support was essentially shifted over to help the Chamorro government when they took office in May of 1990 (Borge 1992: 10). In an office set up in the American Embassy, Janet Ballantyne, in her capacity as director of USAID in Nicaragua, set many of the essential policy guidelines for the new government. The AID mission was able to gain considerable leverage through two mechanisms: (i) agreements concerning aid were tied to certain acts by the government; and (ii) aid dispersals were regulated in a manner which put teeth into policy guidelines for the new government. The largest part of the money went to the Central Bank to finance foreign exchange for the government and private industry. The government had to pay servicing charges on international debts and to cover balance-of-payments shortfalls. Almost $200 million went to the Central Bank in the first year and this money helped to stabilize the currency so that the runaway inflation could be countered. This funding left a limited amount for reconstruction and development programs but essentially all of the project aid was used in very political ways.

Since one of the major goals of the initial AID program was stabilization of the currency, and the largest part of aid going to Nicaragua went to the Central Bank, control over finance was critical. Not only were the majority of funds allocated to the Central Bank, there were also personnel from the United States working at the Bank, in an advisory capacity. One such advisor, for example, was in charge of a newsletter which was distributed to United States business interests advising them about business opportunities in Nicaragua. Her opinion was that business investment depended on a more stable environment than existed in the country under Chamorro and that politics would have to be more secure and stable for her to recommend that US business invest in Nicaragua in 1991. This editor was impatient with the centrist politics of the Chamorro government in 1991 and wanted faster privatization of the banking system (Weiss 1991). The slow rate of dispersal of funds by AID to UNO in 1990 and 1991 indicated that a 'wait and see' perspective was the general policy. Many bureaucratic factors were blamed for this holdup of funds in a US Government Accounting Office report, but the probity of the policy of using the USAID purse strings to force government reforms was not questioned (US GAO 1992: 18–19).

Most of the project aid from USAID was spent to pay for activities related to various aspects of structural adjustment goals. For example, technical assistance for a program for privatization of government-held industries was provided for and the US government financed an Occupational Reconversion Plan for shrinking the size of government. Under this plan, volunteers resigned their jobs for a lump-sum payment of 2000 cordobas which they were supposed to invest in some productive enterprise in the (already overcrowded) informal sector of the economy.

Funds for employment generation were funneled through the Emergency Social Investment Fund (FISE) and they were distributed in an politically interesting way. In the Managua area, for example, men from twelve neighborhoods that had supported the right-wing mayor of Managua, Arnoldo Aleman, were recruited to do the construction work on roads and buildings. Since many construction workers belonging to Sandinista unions and living in pro-Sandinista Barrios were without jobs, the political effectiveness of the right wing could be 'proven' with this kind of spending of money from the United States. Politically motivated use of US aid was a good way for Aleman, and other conservative mayors, to solidify their base and to build further support for their future political endeavors.

Another example of political use of funds for right wing purposes was the $12 million which went to a new textbook program in the first year of US aid. A rapid shift of ideology was considered so important that new textbooks with the correct political slant were immediately purchased with AID funds. Janet Ballantyne defended this expense by saying that she believed that it was very important 'to reestablish civics and morals' in a country that had legalized unilateral divorce (Quandt 1991: 50). The new textbooks contained the traditional Catholic prohibitions against divorce and abortion. Aid also funded, directly and indirectly, a redirection of religious education away from Catholicism guided by liberation theology and back to a traditionalist Catholic interpretation. Cardinal Obando y Bravo's Salesian church received $1.7 million to directly support their vocational education project. According to a Government Accounting Office report, there were questions about implementation of the project which held up dispersal of funds for a period (US GAO 1992: 30–1).

Right-wing religious groups were formed to combat the socialist values developed within the Catholic church because of the close links between the Sandinistas and liberation theologists. A 'City of God' group was formed for the purpose of promoting traditional religious values in Nicaragua. This group included many of the ministers and high-ranking officials of the Chamorro government. The National Endowment for Democracy (NED) sponsored Via Critica, a civic organization which held conferences for conservative mayors. NED also funded right wing radio stations which attacked the government's accommodations with the Sandinistas. Another area of priority aid funding was in the establishment of various alternatives to Sandinista trade unions. AID worked with the AFL/CIO group American Institute for Free Labor Development (AFELD) in funding the development of trade union alternatives to Sandinista unions. The amount spent for this purpose in the first year and a half was $3.5 million (US GAO 1992: 34).

The power of conditionality

The general structural adjustment conditions for USAID and IMF/World Bank aid included privatization, liberalization of trade laws, export orientation, government fiscal austerity and stabilizing the currency. But these extremely difficult adjustments were only part of the story. USAID financed about a third of the central government budget and political and economic conditionality was so powerful in influencing specific policy formulation that USAID could be considered the 'other' governmental power throughout this period (Orellana and Morales 1991: 28–33).

The flow of aid was used to determine both the content and the pace of carrying out very specific government policies. For example, USAID promised to release $5 million 'upon receipt of evidence that a total of 5,000 government employees had left the public sector and that total public sector civilian employment had declined by a corresponding number' (Ferguson 1991: 1). For this level of specificity in policy control, direct links were made between USAID and the various government ministries, without the necessity of communications going through upper level government officials (Orellana and Morales 1991: 32).

In agricultural policy, also, USAID formulated very specific strategies which they believed were necessary in order to 'correct ... negative policies' (USAID 1991: 18). Controls on basic food prices had created distortions from the correct market-oriented pricing policy, from the point of view of USAID officials. Reliance on market pricing was nevertheless not consistently followed in USAID's own policies. In fact, USAID policies often disrupted private markets. For instance, US exports of donated basic grains to Nicaragua reduced prices received for these commodities by Nicaraguan farmers, who reacted to the low prices by reducing production of these necessities (Ferguson 1991: 9).

Industrial self-sufficiency was also sometimes hurt by USAID requirements that the imported products and the services purchased with USAID funds must come from the US. A small Nicaraguan insulator manufacturer, for example, had their contract canceled when a USAID agreement with the Nicaraguan electric company required that the insulators must be purchased in the US (ibid.: 8). This 'tied aid' stipulation regarding inputs also led to US consultants being hired to advise on and evaluate programs and policies that Nicaraguans had a clear comparative advantage in understanding and appraising. An increasing number of people from the United States involved in policy formulation and evaluation mushroomed the group of aid personnel and USAID contractors that were developing policy in Managua.

The Central American Institute for the Administration of Enterprises (INCAE), a Central American business school, was critically important to the new economic policies of UNO. INCAE personnel advised the Nicaraguan government on privatization and monetary policies and developed short business courses and seminars. Contracts with USAID brought together personnel who worked for USAID directly and personnel from the United States who were hired by the school to service contracts and do related work.[3] INCAE was also a center for policy advisement for the Chamorro government. The overall politics of the school did not differ greatly from business administration schools in the United States, ranging from the center to the right with a strong private market orientation. These politics were quite different from and very much to the right of the other intellectual centers in Nicaragua like the University of Central America and the National University.

Reverse land reform

One of the major USAID priorities was a resettlement program for former Contra soldiers which cost $61 million. Since resettlement was often on marginal land and it sometimes did not include sufficient inputs, there was dissatisfaction with the results. Soldiers on both sides remained armed and, as a consequence, violence in the countryside grew because of the inadequate land settlement policy and the poverty resulting from other associated economic policies which limited lending and growth. Reconstituted Contra groups and bands of thieves began to ravage the countryside, making security in rural areas in the early 1990s often worse than during the war years.

The focal point of UNO and AID's attempts to revive agricultural production was cotton. Large farms were returned to former owners and to owners who had stayed in Nicaragua but had not maintained their properties. They were rewarded by the new government with subsidized credit. Meanwhile, cooperatives and small and medium farmers were not able to obtain credit for their investments (*Envio* 1991b: 31–2). In addition to these problems, PL480 US agricultural gifts to Nicaragua worth $57 million included commodities not produced in Nicaragua like wheat and tallow as well as locally produced commodities like rice and corn. Farm incomes decreased because these imports from the US decreased the prices received by local farmers. Following farmer protests, the corn imports were eliminated (USAID 1991).

The perspective of many former landowners returning to Nicaragua was that they would get back 'their' land by one means or another. Some land was judged wrongly confiscated and it was returned rapidly. Other land could be re-accumulated as the result of market processes. Rich Nicaraguans believed that *campesinos* would inevitably make poor market decisions and would, consequently, lose the land they had come to possess. Then, the more market-savvy former owners would be able to grab the land back.

When Arnoldo Alemán, the right-wing former mayor of Managua, gained the presidency in 1997 and tried to enforce a new property policy in the countryside, a surprising new coalition of forces developed to blockade transportation until the president promised to maintain *campesino* property rights. Both former Contras and small owners, who had received land in Sandinista land reforms, protested against the new policies, but the regions in which Contras had settled in were the sites of the strongest protests (*Barricada International* 1997: 6).

Conclusion

The overall effect of the political and economic changes instituted in the first few years after the UNO victory was to shift the access to resources of Nicaraguan society in an upward direction. Priorities of the new government were very different and were often expressed in terms of what the country could or could not 'afford'. The country could no longer afford a good health care system, so that hospitals were shut down in the early 1990s. Fees were increased in public schools and universities and there were even proposals to charge tuition in all public schools. Meanwhile, there were stylish new commodities available such as fashionable garments from the US. There were new aerobics classes, and the private construction industry was booming, funded in part by USAID and in part by new arrivals from Miami.

On the other hand, because of the Central Bank's anti-inflationary 'tight money' policy, unemployment was rampant, with 30 to 50 per cent of the labor force unemployed or underemployed. There was very little money for investment, except for the financing coming from AID and a few returning and foreign investors. Although some domestic industries, such as beer and soft drinks, were reopened with agreements between returning owners and workers, other industries, such as the textile industry, were shut down and thousands of women textile workers lost their jobs.

In the mid-1990s the economy began a modest recovery and GDP started to grow between 2 and 3 per cent per year, still much less than USAID advisers had predicted in 1991 (USAID 1991). Although

US intervention and US aid were the only recourse after the collapse of the Soviet bloc, the expected advantages of market reforms did not materialize in Nicaragua. In El Salvador, the picture was somewhat better. Growth rates have been higher and recovery began in the early 1990s. Strong, indigenous leadership has not appeared in these countries and human resources have not yet been developed. As we will see in the next chapter, the picture was very different in Costa Rica where strong, social-democratic leadership focused on human development and local growth, despite opposing pressures from US aid agencies.

Notes

1. Social-democratic union leaders (UCS) reported these problems in accounting for production in interviews with Nan Wiegersma and Nola Reinhardt in July 1988.
2. In this conflictive political environment, international aid funding in support of the programs agreed to in the Central American Peace Accords has not, in general, been forthcoming. Many European countries have preferred to finance nongovernmental organizations rather than to participate in institution building being financed by the US and international agencies. Their funding preferences have reflected their healthy skepticism about the government's willingness to support broad-based development programs which would include (former) opposition communities (Boyce 1995: 2105–6).
3. INCAE is affiliated with Harvard University and it began as a project connected with the Alliance for Progress in the sixties. Nan Wiegersma spent a Fulbright semester there in 1991.

7
Costa Rican Aid

Introduction

In many respects Costa Rica's economic and cultural environment differs from those in East Asia. In addition, the world market environment has been severely restrictive in the years during Costa Rica's emergence. The past twenty years, for example, have included the debt crisis of the 1980s and structural adjustments in the 1980s and 1990s. During this period, however, Costa Rica has resisted forces that have devastated many other Latin American countries. Costa Rican growth rates have been slower than growth rates of the Asian NICs, but they were higher than most Latin American countries. Costa Rica started at a higher level of development than the Asian NICs because of the social democratic institutions and policies maintained there since the 1950s. Growth rates increased in the late 1980s and early 1990s, before falling during the mid-1990s recession.

Costa Rica can rightly be considered an economic development success that has benefitted from significant amounts of external aid. First, Costa Rica experienced positive per capita growth in the 1980s, although that decade was disastrous for most countries in Latin America. Costa Rica's per capita income and their 'human development index' are now similar to Korean statistics and slightly lower than Taiwan's (*United Nations Human Development Report* 1994–8). Second, Costa Rica has the same kind of commitment to human resource development as exists in the Asian 'tigers', such as Taiwan and South Korea. Third, Costa Rican leaders oversaw several decades of successful development previous to United States involvement, and they were resistant to the usurpation of development decision making during the decade of United States intervention. Finally, Costa Rica's distribution of income and wealth is similar to the Asian NICs.

United States aid to Costa Rica was significant for only a decade (1983 to 1993), one that was fraught with political struggle. From an economic development point of view, however, US aid was successful in helping Costa Rica weather political-economic hardships and in continuing on a capitalist growth path by developing a stronger international trade sector that complemented its domestic institutions and industries.

Historical and geographical preconditions

Costa Rica was a backwater area during the years of Spanish colonialism because of the lack of precious metals found there. Costa Rica was also colonized late, in the late sixteenth century, after certain safeguards had been imposed by Spain concerning the use of indians and slaves as workers. The feudal or seignorial system which had been exported to other Latin American countries was breaking down at the time of Costa Rican colonization and the legal structure of labor relations were changing reflecting a later stage of merchant capitalist influence. The result was that on the Central Valley of Costa Rica, where three-quarters of the immigrants settled, yeoman family farming was the rule because labor for the development of estate farming was scarce.

In the other regions of Costa Rica, those with plantation and *hacienda* agriculture, the workforce was also restricted in numbers in comparison with surrounding countries. *Hacienda* agriculture developed in the North, in Guanacaste Province and in the Atlantic Basin around different export products – for example, beef cattle, bananas and cotton. These farms became large, mostly because of the type of export products produced there. Elsewhere basic grains and vegetable crops were produced on a smaller scale, mostly for the domestic market.

The most important export crop, coffee, developed as a special case. In the nineteenth century, an oligarchy emerged in the Central plateau by buying up land in areas which previously had been farmed by families in order to plant coffee. Although this transition brought a great deal more inequality than previously existed, continued labor shortage in the area prevented the same type of extremely unequal and oppressive conditions which existed in other Latin American countries and in pre-reform Asian countries (Stone 1989: 21–3).

The rise of a modernizing elite

The coffee oligarchy in the late nineteenth century was the motor for Costa Rican economic expansion. Coffee production started in Costa Rica in 1821 and grew rapidly when direct access to European markets was attained in 1845. Coffee exports expanded quickly, bringing in resources which spurred generalized economic growth. Even though a landless laboring class developed among those farmers who were displaced in the process of development of coffee farms on the Central Plain, they nevertheless did not become poverty stricken because rapid growth kept rural unemployment low and real wages relatively high. In addition, by utilizing increased tax revenues from the coffee boom, the coffee elite was able to found an effective bureaucracy in Costa Rica. This bureaucracy carried out nationwide programs to establish formal democracy with periodic elections, a secular education system for the citizenry and permitted the conditions for a free press.

Laissez-faire liberalism took hold in Costa Rica in the first third of the nineteenth-century and continued until twentieth-century political reformers came to power after WWII. Costa Rican liberalism nevertheless favored limits on the power of the military and the church. The influx of foreign capital, however, like the United Fruit Company, into the rural areas eventually took a toll on political stability. Costa Rican workers organized unions to resist the poor working conditions set up by the US companies. Economic insecurity developed also from another aspect of international market integration, the overreliance on a few variable international agricultural markets: coffee, bananas and beef. When prices for these few specialized agricultural goods declined on world markets, a new economic vulnerability became obvious since the population as a whole suffered.

The modern social-democratic state

Widespread political organizing for change did not occur, despite economic and political vulnerabilities, until the twentieth century when economic disasters and loss of markets from the great depression and World War II created conditions for political change. The first reformer of the 1940s was Rafael Calderon, an unlikely politician with unlikely allies. He did not directly challenge the power of the coffee elite, of which he was a part, nevertheless, members of his class felt threatened by the redistributive nature of his reforms. He had a paternalistic perspective typical of the Costa Rican elite, and his reforms included a social security program for the poor, old and ill and a progressive labor code. The church, which was supportive of his social reformist goals, allied with him. His most surprising allies were the members of the Communist Party who took a 'popular front' ideological direction in this period, because of European politics, by allying with this reformer.

When Calderon, with his church and Communist Party backing, ran for a second term, a conservative candidate, Otilio Ultate, won. He was suspected of electoral fraud by the legislature, which was still Calderonist, and this legislature refused to declare Ultate the winner. At this time of confusion and conflict, José Figueres was the leader of an anti-Calderonist social-democratic opposition movement that was more actively progressive than the pro-Calderon communists. The social-democratic group wanted to reshape society and the economy in capitalistic, but also modern and progressive ways. Figueres chose this period of political uncertainty to lead an armed insurrection against the government. This insurrection was not initially completely successful, since the revolutionaries were forced into a compromise with the conservatives because of the threat of intervention from a neighboring dictator, Anastasio Somoza, who would be helped by his United States supporters. The compromise worked out allowed for a Figueres junta to rule for eighteen months, after which Ultate would take power. Figueres used his eighteen months to make several popular changes such as the dissolving of the Costa Rican military. He then ceded power to Ultate and used the period before the next election to build his National Liberation Party into a dominant political force in Costa Rican politics.

Costa Rican state capitalism

Figueres dramatically set the stage for an interventionist social-democratic state by dissolving the army in December of 1948. He turned the fortress keys over to the minister of education, pounding the stone wall to begin the renovation which turned the miliary barracks into a national museum. The social-democratic revolution-aries were interested in setting up the institutional framework for the advancement of the middle class of professionals, small business and bureaucrats at the expense of other classes including the coffee and banana exporters. Social welfare programs that built on the Calderonist base were established in education and health. Figueres quickly nationalized the banking system, subsidizing credit through the state to stimulate new kinds of business development such as agricultural processing and services. Once the Central American Common Market was established in the 1960s, tax breaks and pro-tectionism also stimulated industries, like textiles and garment, to produce for the regional market.

During the decades of the 1950s, 1960s and 1970s an extensive government bureaucracy developed in Costa Rica with government departments and autonomous institutions increasing in size and number, reflecting the social-democratic government's attempts to deal with the social issues which arose in the process of capitalist development. The government workforce grew to one in six by the early 1980s. The expansion of autonomous institutions was particu-larly rapid because of the Costa Rican inclination for solving polit-ical/social issues like child welfare and housing problems by creating autonomous institutions. There were eight of these in 1955, and they increased to 180 in 1979 (Garita 1989: 39–40).

In the 1970s, the state added to the diversification of industry by setting up its own industrial and service enterprises under the Costa Rican Development Corporation known as CODESA. The original purpose of CODESA was to invest capital in industries where private industry could not or would not invest. These industries were sup-posed to be sold to private capitalists (as in the Asian model). In fact, these industries were not transferred from the state sector until the 1980s privatization sponsored by international lending organ-izations forced their transfer (Vega 1989: 140–4).

Other industries were nationalized outright. For example, the Costa Rican Oil Refinery was nationalized in the early 1970s as a result of the oil crisis. A Costa Rican Electricity Institute was formed which gradually absorbed all foreign-owned utilities. Telegraph and telephone service as well as electricity were placed under the control of this institute. An expanding energy source was thus established which was given the task of keeping pace with development in other industries.

The import-substitution phase of Cost Rica's economic develop-ment was successful and Costa Rican growth rates throughout the 1960s and into the 1970s were the highest in Latin America. Manufacturing increased by ten times in value in the period from 1955 to 1975 and the manufacturing labor force increased from 20,000 in 1950 to 60,000 in the mid-1970s (Hall 1985: 230). Industrial production as a percentage of GDP reached 29 per cent by 1973 and industrial exports increased to 27 per cent of total exports. Export growth to Central American Common Market countries was particularly important (Rodríguez 1993: 4). By the end of the 1970s, Costa Rica's import-substitution policies had developed an indus-trial sector composed of light consumer and intermediate goods industry rather than heavy machine tool and machinery industry. This type of manufacturing reflected Costa Rica's possibilities as a small country with limited but expanding markets in the region. Domestic industries included clothing and textiles, cosmetics, food, drink and tobacco, small electrical appliances, pharmaceutical, printing and publishing, and paint and fertilizer made from petro-leum. Although three-quarters of industries were producing con-sumer goods, most factories were more capital- than labor-intensive. Capital goods industries were primarily for the production or assem-bly of imported parts for cars and equipment. Most tools and equip-ment used for production were imported (Hall 1985: 330–5).

The expansion of the role of government through CODESA in the 1970s led to political controversy because there were areas where CODESA had started competing with the private sector and there were political groups opposed to this. Many industrialists who had originally supported the development of this semi-autonomous gov-ernment agency became unhappy with its growth into those areas that were not merely complementary with private industry but were competitive with existing domestic industry (Vega 1989: 143). Some specific private markets which the public sector had newly entered were the cement and aluminum industries, and tourism. The political movements opposed to government intervention in these areas helped to set the stage for 1980s restructuring and privatization.

Contemporary agriculture: land tenure and reform

Costa Rica still has considerable uncultivated land area which could be brought into production. The relatively equal distribution of income and property in the country and the advantaged position of Costa Rican workers and farmers partly reflects the average Costa Rican's possibilities for access to property. Squatters' settlements on uncultivated areas have been tolerated and eventually legitimized throughout most of Costa Rican history. Nevertheless, new ideas about the restrictions of ownership of uncultivated land have recently become more significant. During the 1960s the practice of land occupation began to be actively discouraged. The more traditional rights of peasants to cultivate unused land were sometimes dismissed in favor of modern ownership rights of the landowners to hold land out of cultivation. Along with this policy change, various land reform programs were developed in order to solve the continuing problem of landlessness among portions of the peasant population. Some programs brought unused land into production, while others developed agricultural cooperatives and there was some land transferred to small cultivators.

Despite these reform programs, land occupations increased in the period after 1980 because of economic crises and hard times for rural workers. In the contemporary period, approximately half the families in rural areas do not own land – most of these people work for owners of large farms. A portion of these workers periodically seek to locate land that their families could till.

The cutting of government support for basic grain prices, as part of the 1980s structural adjustment policies imposed on Costa Rica by the international aid community, led to considerable hardship among farmers. Groups of farmers organized demonstrations in San Jose because US Food for Peace donations unfairly affected the prices that they were paid for their products. Marginal farmers and landless laborers were particularly affected by the removal of price supports. Some of these farmers turned to land occupations in order to gain cultivatable area so that they could make ends meet. Although historically most land occupations have been in remote regions, since 1980 land occupations have increasingly been in the more settled privately owned, but unused, areas. When security forces have tried to remove peasants from occupied land in Costa Rica, community and church support for the peasant farmers have sometimes pushed the government to back down (Barry 1987: 150–3). Communities often support the traditional rights of peasants to cultivate unused land over modern ownership rights, but increasingly in the contemporary period, farmers are forced from land they try to occupy.

The debt crisis and restructuring in the 1980s

Debt crises in the 1980s in Latin America have partly resulted from the phenomenon of larger amounts of credit and smaller grants in US aid packages compared to US aid to Asian countries. In addition, a larger portion of market rate loans caused problems. As we explained in Chapter 2, loan portions of US aid packages rose beginning in the late 1950s and then rose again with the Alliance for Progress aid of the 1960s to Latin America. Since the 1960s, debts owed to the World Bank and the International Monetary Fund have also increased dramatically. The higher incidence of loans as part of aid packages weighed especially heavily on aid recipients as real interest rates increased in the 1980s.

In addition to their international public debt burden, Costa Rican external debt expanded dramatically in the 1970s when US commercial banks with excess liquidity (mainly because of bank deposits of oil revenues from the Middle East) lent large amounts of dollars to Costa Rica because of their relative growth record and reputation for political stability. By the early 1980s, Costa Rica had accumulated public external debt which was greater than their annual GDP and an unusually high percentage of this debt was owed to commercial banks. The public debt service for Costa Rica had grown to nearly half of the annual value of exports by the early 1980s. Costa Rica declared a moratorium on external debt payments in August 1981 (before many other countries in analogous circumstances took similar actions in that next period). The high percentage of short term private debt contracted in the late seventies had put Costa Rica in a particularly vulnerable position. The coincidence of this debt crisis with the Central American political upheaval aggravated the overall debt problem. Central American markets for Costa Rican products decreased or were eliminated by the collapse of the Common Market. Ultimately, however, the interest of the United States in influencing Costa Rica politically, led to a greater availability of US dollars for Costa Rican development which eased their debt situation.

The financial crises of the late 1970s and early 1980s were also the related to short-term price changes. Traditional exports such as coffee and sugar had decreased in price relative to Costa Rican imports so that Costa Rican terms of trade turned strongly negative in the late 1970s. During the same period energy price increases also raised the cost of oil imports considerably. Rapid inflation and falling real wages in 1980–1 led to the political will, with the 1982 election of Luis Alberto Monge (PLN), to undertake serious financial reform. The initial focus of reform was on monetary stability with the other aspect of restructuring, such as liberalizing of the economy, put off. There was a financial 'shock treatment' to end inflation. Monetary expansion, the interest rate and public expenditure were pegged in real terms, while price controls were established at the expected rate of inflation.

The exchange rate was brought under control by strict regulation of the Central Bank. Henceforth, expected mini-devaluations aimed at maintaining the value of the colon relative to the major trading partners (Rodríguez 1993: 10). Inflation and exchange rate variations were rapidly brought under control with these measures. Then, within a new environment of monetary stability, the government could go on to other international financial issues and liberalization of the economy. Costa Rica deviated from the IMF/World Bank's more drastic (orthodox) approach to restructuring their economy and chose a more slowly paced and flexible (heterodox) adjustment program. This was possible at least partly because of the financing available from USAID. The US, because of strategic interests in Costa Rica, moved quickly and insured that the structural adjustment program was negotiated through USAID and the Inter-American Development Bank rather than the IMF/World Bank (ibid.: 18).

The renegotiation of terms with the international financial community was very difficult for all of the Latin American countries affected by the debt crisis. Costa Rica suffered, like others, from the outside imposition of economic reforms which were often renegotiated throughout the eighties and were conditioned upon their debt. Nevertheless, Costa Rica was able to negotiate deals which were more favorable than the average restructuring arrangements. The successful development of nontraditional exports for sale to US markets and the considerable additional funds made available to Costa Rica made their difficult situation more financially possible to manage.

Costa Rica was eventually able to shift her debt portfolio to a more normal debt structure, with the largest portion of debt owed to multinational agencies and a small portion (20 per cent) to private banks. This shift was largely the result of a scheme developed during the Brady Initiative to resolve the remaining Latin American debt crisis issues. In 1990, Costa Rica bought back some of her debt at 16 cents to the dollar and exchanged some for long-term government bonds. Costa Rica then agreed to regular payment of debt service arrears. The financing of this agreement came from bilateral aid funds from the US, Japan, Taiwan and Canada, in addition to loans from the World Bank and the IMF. This financial deal was considered the best negotiated by any country during the Brady Initiative (ibid.: 22).

The cost of bailout: structural adjustments

Other structural adjustments started in Costa Rica almost two years after the initial monetary stabilization measures were begun. When they began, there was very little flexibility concerning the tightly drawn program of conditions upon which USAID and the IMF/World Bank insisted. Privatization and liberalization of the economy were nonnegotiable terms. Adjustments which the Costa Ricans accepted without too much argument included a reduction of the public sector in size and in market influence. There was a freeze put on public employment and the fiscal deficit was reduced drastically from 19 per cent of the budget to 14 per cent and then to 7 per cent the next year. A plan for the divestment of many CODESA firms was also accepted with little argument (ibid.: 11–12).

Liberalization of the market meant a drastic change in the strategy of self-sufficiency in agriculture adopted during the import-substitution period. Price controls and subsidies for agricultural products allowed for higher farm prices, but subsidized consumer prices were abandoned. Internal agricultural prices were allowed to move toward world market prices with the resulting farmer discontent discussed in the previous section.

There was considerably more argument over the pace of the trade liberalization process, than over its content. Costa Rican officials argued for gradualism and their perspective on this issue was finally adopted in their multilateral negotiations with aid agencies. As shown in the next section, Costa Rican officials were interested in giving incentives in order to develop new export markets. They also wanted to protect the domestic industries set up in the earlier period from abrupt and potentially destructive changes. More gradual changes in tariffs on imported goods were proposed by Costa Rican leaders because they were deemed essential for protection against deindustrialization of domestic industries.

The benefits of aid: trade advantages

The Caribbean Basin Initiative was important in helping Costa Rica to recover economically. The United States market was made available for Costa Rican agricultural and industrial producers, free of import taxes. Although textiles and garments were exempt from the Initiative, these 'nontraditional' exports were encouraged through the General System of Preferences. The more important advantage for Costa Rica, however, with respect to garment manufacture, was that garment quotas for East Asian manufactures were threatening to restrict further imports. It was to the advantage of Asian manufacturers to shift final assembly tasks to Central American free trade zones in order for these products to enter the US under Central American, not Asian, quotas.

Although traditional exports to the US like coffee and sugar faced declining prices during the 1980s, the Costa Rican/USA program to encourage new exports was so successful as to make up for this loss in revenues. Costa Rica benefitted more than other countries from the CBI because of their expanding level of trade. One technique used for setting up Costa Rican export processing for the US market was for AID financed investment officers to use the Dun and Bradstreet Listings of American Corporations. They would pinpoint the labor intensive industrial processes and then attempt to sell the firm on producing in Costa Rica (Honey 1994: 128). Thus, USAID promoted Costa Rican integration into the international economy by attempting to move production units, and jobs, to Costa Rica.

Costa Rica successfully resisted the orthodox neoliberal competitive model favored by international institutions like the IMF and the World Bank, and the Reagan–Bush administrations' aid programs to Costa Rica (1980–92). Costa Rica instead supported a more slowly paced and heterodox approach toward a greater interdependence with the world market. The Costa Rican government was directed by USAID, the World Bank and the International Monetary Fund, in accordance with their structural adjustment program, to shift away from her import-substitution program and, instead, promote exports in the 1980s. As a result, the country embarked on a program of compensatory programs to encourage its export sector, while continuing to partially protect its domestic industries.

Instead of eliminating trade barriers, taxes and subsidies, Costa Rica shifted their mix and redirected their benefits to transnational companies (TNCs) and the younger workers they employed. In the period when import substitution had been more popular in development planning, Costa Rica had set more conditions on investments coming from the TNCs. The trade, labor and investment regulations then favored domestic industries, and protected national interests. More recently, with Costa Rica under orders from the IMF and the World Bank to 'liberalize trade,' the legislated deviations from competition have run in a different direction, favoring the TNCs over national firms and favoring the younger and less experienced laborers working in export processing. For example, the special incentives – such as reduced rents and reduced taxes – that were offered to export processors gave them a competitive advantage over domestic corporations producing for the home market.

The Certificado de Abono Tributario granted credits against import taxes for the nontraditional export sector in Costa Rica. This incentive initiative was added to programs which gave special advantages to companies producing in Free Trade Zones beginning in 1981 and to other *maquila* (export-processing) advantages which began in 1976. Meanwhile, in accordance with the World Bank trade liberalization program, tariffs on imports were reduced from a range of 0 to 100 per cent to from 5 to 40 per cent. Raw materials and capital goods were given the smallest import duties and finished goods the highest. The textile and garment industry was specifically exempted from this World Bank accord, however, and import tax reductions in this industry were put off for a future time.

The special treatment of *maquila* industries compensated for the import taxes that were kept in force in order to protect domestic industry. The goal of the 'compensating market deviations' was to liberalize the market. Although a generalized dispensation from import taxes for all raw materials and intermediate goods might, in fact, have been a move in the direction of liberalization, favors for particular industries did not really move the economy in that direction. Despite the failure to liberalize, or perhaps because of it, the drive to encourage garment and electronics manufacture was successful because the trade advantages increased markets for export to the United States.

The special exceptions and changes in labor legislation in Costa Rica's *maquila* industries also did not move the country towards a free-market economy, but instead further favored transnational corporations. For example, the general labor regulation which restricted night work for women, was lifted for the TNCs operating in free trade zones but remained in force elsewhere. Another exemption involved periods of apprenticeship or probation, when workers could be paid less than the legal minimum in wages and/or social insurance taxes and benefits could be foregone. This regulation encouraged the employer to fire the employee after the apprenticeship or probational period.[1] These exemptions encouraged firms to first hire inexperienced girls for a six-month period and then fire them when the probational term was over and hire a new group of probational employees (Guzman 1984: 11). Therefore, experienced workers were put at a disadvantage because of the law.

The TNCs, which in the 1970s had been restricted in their removal of profits and investment from Costa Rica and other less developed countries, were encouraged in the 1990s to move from one nation's free trade zone to another's when their tax 'vacations' were over. Other factors which promoted frequent moving included increased relative wage rates or better benefits packages offered in other countries. Increasing wage rates in Costa Rica, caused by the success of their development program, have led to such moves. A case in point was the precipitous closing of the El Roble plant. The

380 employees were surprised when they arrived at work on 8 August 1991 to find the plant closed without advance warning and with back wages owed (Mora 1991: 5A).

The Costa Rican government gave special advantages to *maquila* firms during the economic crisis of the 1980s, in order to build export markets rapidly. The shift, however, did not produce a *maquila*-dominated economy. Costa Rican policy makers understood the limits of *maquila* industries, so the Costa Rican development process did not become overly dependent on them. The strong justification for a diversified development plan that does not rely on *maquilas* is expressed a Costa Rican business journal:

> ... the maquila is a very important component of export activity Nevertheless, it is known internationally that one of the greatest problems of the maquila firms is the small aggregate value that stays in the country and is translated into payment of public salaries, and with the additional aggravation that at any moment the enterprize can leave and go to other countries. (*Panorama International* 1991: 9)[2]

The garment and textile industries in Costa Rica include firms that participate in international markets, but are not *maquila* firms. In addition, there are more than 50 enterprises which produce solely for the local market and thousands of small household producers who either subcontract to larger enterprises or vend their own products (*Panorama International* 1991: 9).

Garment industry subcontracting usually has several layers and Costa Rican firms often fulfill contracts for part of the international production process which then continues in, for example, the Dominican Republic or Puerto Rico. Approximately 50 associations and cooperatives of women clothing makers in Costa Rica contract-out to the international firms (Vanolli 1991). There are also numerous examples of internal subcontracting within Costa Rica. The government has encouraged the international garment industry to make backward linkages, which are frequently *not* made in other countries, to Costa Rican *maquila* enterprises. The garment component of the Costa Rican *maquila* program, however, has been on the decline for some time. The advantages for firms investing in Costa Rica in the 1970s and 1980s were skilled labor and political stability.

The disadvantages of such investment in Costa Rica, as compared to other Central American countries, have increased over time. These disadvantages include relatively high salaries and social security costs and additional transportation costs from the more dispersed processing zones. Investors have been able to find less expensive garment workers in other parts of Central America and the Caribbean. Partly as a result, more technologically developed industries are gradually replacing garment companies. In the Cartago Free Trade Zone, for example, during the period 1985 to 1991, the garment component of the zone decreased from approximately 80 to 50 per cent (Zamora 1991).

The Costa Rican reforms burdened some sectors of the population and increased inequality for others, but they also successfully provided trade advantages in an increasingly interdependent world market. Figure 7.1 shows the relative effects of the trade advantages which were much more successfully engineered in Costa Rica than in other Central American Countries. By the late 1980s, exports from Costa Rica to the US were outpacing those of other Central American countries. This advantage continued to increase after the US Aid Program was discontinued in 1992.

Thus, the 1980s Costa Rican export promotion programs were, on balance, successful. In the course of the decade, nontraditional exports nearly doubled, reaching $655 million by the end of the decade and industrial exports increased by 50 per cent, to $466 million. Agricultural nontraditionals were also very successful, increasing by almost 300 per cent to $132 million and agroindustrial exports increased to $57 million (Salazar 1990: 259).

Conclusion: the end of US aid and the parallel state

The Costa Rican 'production for export' model, developed with USAID help, has often been lauded by the economic and financial ministers of other Central American countries as well as USAID people in Central America. Costa Rican development success has, in fact, been exceptional for this very unstable part of the world. After a growth slowdown in the beginning to mid-1980s, growth rates and per capita incomes in Costa Rica had started to rise again by the late 1980s (Jiménez 1990: 172–7). Even with cutbacks in aid in the 1990s, the Costa Rican economy continued to grow until the

Figure 7.1 Exports from Central America to the US

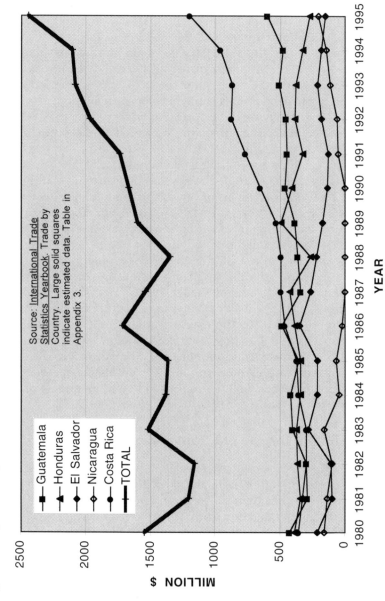

middle of the decade, when recession set in. Although the Costa Rican model is unique in the region, it appears to have worked toward balanced development.

USAID grants to Costa Rica were mostly in the form of economic support funds (ESF) rather than project aid. Utilizing these funds, the US was very active in attempting to influence Costa Rican development policy. USAID attempted the same executive control measures practiced in other countries but the results were quite different. Structural adjustment policies were written into funding agreements with the US and with multilateral agencies. Policy changes were monitored and each time that there was any problem with Costa Rican government policy, the already appropriated aid funds would not be dispersed until the policy shift had been instituted. USAID, in addition, used their money to help set up private banks and private agencies in order to fund their own export development strategy. These banks and agencies were often in direct competition with existing Costa Rican institutions whose tasks were then undercut by USAID. For example, a USAID-financed Coalition for Development Initiatives (CINDE) was set up to do the same job as the government agency with the task of promotion exports, CENPRO. USAID also set up a private bank to help with funding of export investments, and the government banks with the same mission were then ignored.

USAID in Costa Rica organized their projects and their expenditures so as to bypass the legislature whenever possible. Setting up 'private sector' agencies helped in this regard. The legislature had been traditionally very active in development policy and political tensions rose concerning these policy moves by USAID. In the ten year struggle between the Costa Rican government and USAID over a central restructuring condition, that of privatizing CODESA, the limits of what actually was possible helped to constrain the grand changes for which USAID was pushing. After a political battle to get a divestiture act through the legislature, USAID worked behind the scenes with their money and influence in order to get the job done with a minimum of additional problems. USAID set up a trust fund (FINTRA) in order to finance the changes. FINTRA was supposed to buy government firms at their official legal value and then sell them at the price the market would bear.

A great deal of aid money went into transactions such as the following: (i) FINTRA purchased an aluminum fabricating company for

$52 million and eighteen months later sold it for only $7 million; (ii) salaries between $2000 and $3600 a month were paid to board members although several of them devoted only five to eight hours a week to their job; and (iii) 140 trips to look for investors produced no positive results. This wasteful expenditure undermined the divestiture project, but it still struggled along. By 1990, eight CODESA companies had been switched to other government agencies, seven had been sold to private buyers, one had been sold to a cooperative and one had been liquidated while CODESA retained its interests in two (Honey 1994: 108–9). Although the imposed privatization was resisted by many Costa Ricans, the willingness of USAID to pay for the process and to settle for carrying out only half of the program made the transition much easier and less costly to Costa Rica than it was for other Latin American countries who often were forced by the IMF to sell their assets at bargain prices to TNCs.

Before and during the Oscar Arias administration, there had been considerable criticism of 'the parallel state' which had been built up by USAID under the Monge government. As the USAID program was winding down in the early 1990s, AID shifted gears and promoted a merger between CINDE and the government agency CENPRO. Since the traditional Central American markets for Costa Rica's products were also opening up again in the 1990s, a single export promotion agency again seemed possible. By the 1990s, aid commitments were shrinking as well so that the Costa Rican government was better able to recoup the power and degrees of freedom that were necessary to plan its own development. The successful Costa Rican experience remains unique in the Western Hemisphere. Many countries would like to replicate their success, but it remains to be seen whether their model can be duplicated in other Latin American countries, most of which have a much more neoliberal basis for their economic policies and lack Costa Rica's experience with successful development planning.

Notes

1. This particular regulation has also been a problem with Free Trade Zone regulations elsewhere (United Nations, *Survey*, 1989: 148).
2. Translation by Nan Wiegersma.

8
Aid Policy Conclusions in an Era of Financial Crisis

The financial crisis in Asia

In 1997 Asia became the site of a financial crisis that spread to threaten markets and economies around the world. Despite the persistently positive economic performance of most East and Southeast Asian countries – characterized by high growth rates, low inflation rates, high private savings, budget surpluses, and strong exports – international currency speculators attacked Asian currencies and provoked a panicked withdrawal of massive amounts of short-term capital. Starting with the Thai baht and spreading to currencies up along the east coast of Asia, affected currencies lost half of their value in less than a year. Stock markets in those countries dropped by about 50 per cent (IMF 1998c). Accustomed to their recent economic successes, many in Asia struggled to understand why the crisis occurred, why it has been so severe and what the implications are for the East Asian model of development.

Ironically, economic success in East and Southeast Asia was, in a sense, a precondition for the financial crisis. High profits in the Asian economies attracted enormous, mostly short-term capital inflows. From 1993 to 1996, Europeans pumped $318 billion, Japanese $260 billion, and the US $46 billion into Asian financial markets in search of quick returns. South Korea received $100 billion of these funds, Thailand received $70 billion, Indonesia $55 billion and China $55 billion to finance long-term, often speculative, building and industrial projects (*FEER* 1998a). The billions of speculative funds came primarily from private lenders. The vast majority of funds were borrowed for less than one year, in foreign currencies, by private banks who, without government oversight, re-lent the funds to speculative, long-term local projects. Initially, this huge influx of money had financed rapid and apparently profitable growth. As excess capacity in real estate and the local service and industrial sectors soared, confidence began to flag concerning whether even rapid increases in exports could pay off the accumulated loans.

Lagging exports to Japan and the US, due to increased competition from China, triggered an investment confidence crisis. This loss of confidence induced speculative runs on the Thai baht and later on other regional currencies. Foreign investors began to withdraw their funds in an increasing panic that pushed down currency values, and lowered stock market and other asset prices. The resulting massive outflows of short-term funds meant that, despite budget and trade surpluses, low inflation and high private savings and strong export performance, the affected Asian economies faced domestic credit crises that threatened the continued viability of otherwise sound businesses.

IMF interventions

The financial crisis in East and Southeast Asia served as an occasion for aggressive interventions by the International Monetary Fund (IMF) into the economic affairs of the region. The currency, stock and real estate market collapses made private lenders reluctant to loan money to businesses in the region. Japan had proposed setting up a US$100 billion rescue fund in 1997 to prevent financial crisis in Asia. At that time the US wanted the IMF in charge of any bailout and reform packages. So, the US Treasury Secretary, Robert Rubin, personally called the IMF General Secretary, Michel Camdessus, to insist that the IMF block the Japanese bailout fund (*New York Times* 2 October 1998). Consequently, later that year the IMF was the only agency able to gather sufficient funds to bail out domestic and international banks and prevent economic depression across the region. IMF officials believed that the crisis was: ' ... exacerbated by governance issues, notably government involvement in the private sector and lack of transparency in corporate and financial accounting and the provision of financial and economic data' (IMF 1998b). The IMF pressed economic reform programs on the affected governments in return for US$113 billion in direct and multilateral loan funds.

The required reforms included (i) the imposition of flexible exchange rates to permit further currency devaluations; (ii) a tightened monetary policy to attempt to slow capital outflows by raising domestic interest rates; (iii) structural reforms to reduce trade barriers and liberalize/open the financial systems; and (iv) reduced government spending to quiet inflation fears. The IMF has explained that forceful, far-reaching structural reforms are at the heart of all the programs, ' ... the centerpiece of the Asian programs has been the comprehensive reform of the financial systems' (IMF 1998b). The financial system reforms also included closing bankrupt financial institutions, requiring local businesses to accept new business partners in order to reduce debt and increasing foreign ownership of domestic financial institutions and businesses.

South Korea

The South Korean economy adjusted to external shocks to its domestic stability in the 1970s and 1980s without suffering financial crises because government agencies regulated financial markets. Government regulation then insured that Korean firms could borrow funds only for productive investments. On the other hand, if firms needed funds to keep their businesses going, the government provided them. When necessary, the Korean government boosted the domestic economy with increased government spending to enable business to continue to meet their financial obligations.

These regulatory safeguards were eliminated when the US government insisted that South Korea had to remove controls over its financial markets in order to join the Organization for Economic Cooperation and Development (OECD) in the early 1990s. In addition to this loss of control, the Korean government was forced to abolish the Economic Planning Board, its major economic strategy institution since the 1960s (Wade and Veneroso 1998). The South Korean government also acceded to US demands to loosen controls on private currency trading. These reforms allowed foreigners to engage in speculative trading in Korean currency. South Korea then had to permit its domestic banks to freely borrow from foreign lenders and to lend to domestic and foreign borrowers without government supervision. These US required 'reforms' severely reduced the Korean government's ability to regulate and protect its economy from destructive external economic events like those that produced the Asian financial crisis.

The US-inspired deregulation of the South Korean financial system allowed the destabilizing short-term foreign currency loans for speculative long-term investments that lay at the heart of the Asian financial crisis. Without government controls or coordination to restrict borrowing to productive investment in low-risk expansion of industrial capacity, debt increased by more than $100 billion. Almost 70 per cent of that money had to be repaid in less than one year. Most of these loans funded speculation in overseas construction and other risky investments. The borrowers were betting that they could obtain low-cost money in time to pay off their existing loans. Instead, all the money that poured into Korea artificially boosted the value of Korea's currency. The overvalued currency made Korea's exported goods more expensive and its industries less profitable (Chang 1997). As financial panics spread amongst foreign investors in the rest of Asia, the South Korean economy was left exposed by its weakened export performance. Speculators' unrestricted sales of South Korea's currency slashed its value and produced a panicked outsurge of the short-term loan money. Businesses were then not able to borrow the money they needed in order to repay their debts. Korea was threatened with economic disaster unless it received immediate external assistance.

At that time the IMF stepped forward to bail out Korean financial agencies and their foreign lenders. In exchange for the funds necessary to quell short-term collapse, the IMF required Korea to adopt low inflation targets, just as its 50 per cent currency devaluation caused the skyrocketing of import prices of nonsubstitutable goods. Within months, food and other consumer prices rose by almost 50 per cent; however, the IMF-imposed inflation targets forced South Korean monetary authorities to severely cut back the amount of money available for loans. With less money to be lent, interest rates doubled to over 20 per cent. Businesses often were neither able to afford these rates nor to otherwise find the money they needed to keep going. Millions of jobs were threatened as the domestic credit crunch pushed thousands of firms towards bankruptcy. In addition, the IMF required the Korean government to reduce its spending.

These spending cutbacks impaired local business activity and worse-ned the economic crisis.

The IMF insisted on additional structural reforms to further restrict Korean government regulation of its commercial banks, to prohibit it from lending directly to Korean firms and to stop it from assisting individual corporations to avoid bankruptcy. It also required wider opening of Korea's capital accounts to enable even freer inflow and outflow of portfolio and direct investment capital (Wade and Veneroso 1998). Thus, the IMF agreement not only dis-assembled Korea's banking system, it also created conditions that allowed foreign capital to begin to buy up South Korea's most profitable industrial assets at 'fire sale' prices. The agreement, for example, lifted the ceiling on individual foreign ownership to over 50 per cent by 1998 and allowed foreign financial firms to purchase domestic financial firms without limitation. In late December 1997, *The Economist* magazine reported Korean press complaints that the IMF's hidden purpose was to open doors for American business (*The Economist* 1997). In mid- 1998, The *Far Eastern Economic Review* (*FEER*) reported a widespread belief in Asia that the financial crisis was managed by the IMF on behalf of the US in order to bankrupt Asian manufacturers and financial firms and to allow American companies to come in and buy up everything cheaply (*FEER* 1998b).

The IMF did not create the financial crisis. It did, however, exploit the crisis to push its policy goals in Asia. In particular, the IMF sought to dismantle the institutional foundations of the East Asian model of development. The rescue and reform plans for South Korea, for example, reorganized the Bank of Korea so that it could no longer function as an independent central bank. They also trans-formed Korea's Ministry of Finance so that its industrial policy cap-abilities were significantly curtailed. IMF reforms made it impossible for these agencies to continue the monetary, credit and interest rate policies that financed South Korea's successful domestic economic development. Why did the IMF want to dismantle the institutions responsible for building the successful Korean version of the 'Asian miracle?' Wade and Veneroso (1998) argued that the answer involves the interests of the owners and managers of international capital: 'The reforms sought by the Fund are connected in one way or another with further opening up Asian economies to interna-tional capital ... '

Wade and Veneroso also asked why the Fund insists on opening the capital accounts of countries that are awash with domestic savings. In addition, they wanted to know why the Fund has done so little by way of organizing debt rescheduling negotiations, preferring to administer bailout funds in return for structural and institutional reforms? Their answer is that a profitable alliance has been formed between Wall Street firms and the US Treasury Department:

> [Wall Street] ... has helped over the past year to push the process of amending the IMF's articles of agreement to require member governments to remove capital controls and adopt full capital account convertiblility. The extended Wall Street-Treasury-IMF complex has likewise worked to promote the World Trade Organization's agreement on liberalizing financial services ... Many developing country governments, including prominently several Asian country ones, opposed the WTO's efforts to liberalize financial services ... Then came the financial crisis ... By December 1997 the Asian leaders agreed to drop their objections, and on 12 December 1997, more than 70 countries signed the agreement that commits them to open banking, insurance and securities markets to foreign firms ... Meanwhile the OECD has been pushing ahead quickly with the negotiation of the Multilateral Agreement on Investment, that liberalizes all direct foreign investment restrictions, requiring signatory governments to grant equal treatment to foreign as to domestic companies. It will preclude many of the policies of the developmental state. (Wade and Veneroso 1998)

In other words, the IMF followed a political agenda to overturn the East Asian model and replace it with a US-inspired 'free-market' approach that privileges international corporations' interests at the expense of national economic development.

Conventional interpretations of the crisis

The 1997–8 Asian financial crisis was seized upon as an opportunity to question, reinterpret and dismantle the East Asian model of development. According to Michel Camdessus, managing director of the IMF, the 'Asian Miracle' was based on saving, prudent fiscal policies, investment in physical and human capital and liberalizing and opening up national economies. In his opinion the miracle had a 'dark side' in that it was plagued by destructive government-- business 'cronyism.' In order to shed light on this dark side, business affairs in the Asian countries should be transacted in an irreproach- able and transparent manner and all forms of corruption, nepotism and favoritism must be shunned. Cronyism and favoritism are the terms that the IMF used to describe the East Asian systems of indica- tive planning and government regulation of, and cooperation with, business that were the foundations of their successful approach to economic development. The IMF portrayed itself as the enlighten- ing, objective force necessary to ensure enactment of reform pro- grams to restore investor confidence and reestablish access to international capital markets. These programs 'go far beyond restor- ing the major fiscal, monetary, or external balances. Their aim is to strengthen financial systems, improve governance and trans- parency, and restore economic competitiveness' (IMF 1998d). The 'reforms' that opened Asian economies to unregulated invasion and buy-outs by foreign capital effectively eliminated their economic sovereignty.

The Clinton administration strongly supported the IMF approach. Janet Yellen, chair of the President's Council of Economic Advisors, argued that the 'fatal flaws of the East Asian economies' are the 'heart of the problems.' She continued by saying that ' ... the crisis countries favored centralized and behind the scenes mechanisms for the allocation of capital ... ' and that ' ... in the long run, reliance on such behind the scenes relationships for capital allocation may lead to increasingly poor investment decisions' (Yellen 1998). Yellen then extended her attack to the Japanese economic model itself by stating: 'Hopefully, the apparent collapse of the Japanese model of capital markets abroad will reinforce Japan's resolve to carry out the structural reforms that are needed to address the long-term prob- lems facing that country' (ibid.). Meanwhile, Robert Rubin, US Secretary of the Treasury, commented:

[t]he financial assistance mobilized by the International Monetary Fund has played a key role in providing breathing room and developing strong reform programs for these countries. What is important now is for sustained adherence to these strong

reform programs ... Sound macroeconomic policies, stronger financial systems, structural reform and more open markets are the key to restoring financial stability and to the long term economic health of these nations... .

Rubin contends, in addition, that there are advantages for the US in turning to the IMF for enforcement of new international regulations:

> [t]he IMF has ... the expertise to shape effective reform programs, the leverage to require a country to accept conditions that no assisting nation could require on its own, and it internationalizes the burden ... Failure to support fully the IMF now could shake confidence in American leadership in the global economy. (Rubin 1998)

Critiques of these conventional interpretations

Jeffrey Sachs, head of the Harvard Institute for International Development, has pointed out that as recently as the summer of 1997, the IMF praised South Korea for its ' ... continued impressive macroeconomic performance' and ' ... enviable fiscal record' (1997). He explained that this pre-crisis approval of Korean economic performance supported the view that there was no 'fundamental' reason for Asia's economic difficulties, other than the financial panic itself. Since Asian countries' budgets were in balance, their inflation rates were low and their export performance was strong, IMF efforts to ' ... impose a severe macroeconomic contraction on top of the market panic' in order to 'calm the markets' was grossly misconceived and will only exacerbate the existing crisis. Sachs stressed that there was no economic justification for the IMF to seize upon Asia's financial crisis as an opportunity to force reforms on the Asian economies.

Allen Meltzer of the Cato Institute explained the crisis as partially a problem of short-term funds being used for long-term investments:

> [private] Asian borrowers used short-term renewable credits from foreign banks to finance long-term loans ... borrowed in foreign currencies ... and loaned in local currency. They accepted the

exchange risk without hedging ... Foreign lenders shared this myopia ... They did not monitor the total assets and liabilities of the borrowers ... These three elementary errors, are evidence of the pervasive problem of moral hazard ... Extending new credit helps the Asian banks to avoid default, but the money goes to the foreign bankers. (Meltzer 1998)

He thus extends the moral hazard analysis, often used against Asian governments, to include foreign creditors. The foreign bankers, who as creditors of Asian banks and companies have an interest in avoiding loan default, have pressured their governments, and through them the IMF, to implement the bailout operations in ways that provide the creditors themselves with multiple benefits. For example, to raise the money to finance the bailouts, the G7 governments issue bonds underwritten by the large investment banks. The increased debt, and interest and fee payments, increases the stranglehold these private lenders have over economic policy (Choussudosky 1997).

In these ways, IMF funds rescued the private foreign lenders whose unregulated lending and currency speculation precipitated the Asian financial crisis. IMF reforms imposed the costs of repayment upon the domestic populations of the Asian countries, instead of on the institutions that were responsible. Meltzer's point about 'moral hazard' is that, if the perpetrators of the crisis are rewarded and others are made to pay, then the risk that crisis conditions will reoccur is increased. Joseph Stiglitz, former chair of the President's Council of Economic Advisors and currently senior vice president and chief economist at the World Bank, contended that the allocation of investment, most notably to speculative real estate, and short-term borrowing were problems that arose due to excessively rapid financial liberalization. He argued that it was unlikely that the crisis could have occurred without the liberalization of capital accounts (Stiglitz 1998b). The IMF reforms increased the likelihood of future crises because they accelerated financial liberalization and the opening of capital markets.

In effect, the IMF, with the cooperation of other international organizations and the support of the US government and US corporations, now acts as a global central bank which regulates the financial systems and economic policies of the international capitalist economy according to the development ideology of the US. The current financial crises in Asia have provided the IMF with an opportunity to restructure Asian economies to fit the rules of the economic development game according to the US model: trade liberalization, open and deregulated financial markets and 'western' accounting, financial and legal practices that favor established, developed country banks and corporations. East Asian countries, including Japan, are resisting many of these attempts to dismantle their model of economic development; however, they have succumbed to others, at the high costs imposed by the 1997 financial crisis.

The consequences of IMF and US intervention

Rapid investment and growth in Asia vastly expanded the productive capacity, especially for exports, of the region. World markets, especially in the US, grew more slowly. Estimated excess capacity, measured in terms of how much capacity would have to be reduced in order for profits to exceed the international cost of capital, ranged from 40 per cent in Thailand and Malaysia to 60 per cent in South Korea and Indonesia. Japan's excess capacity was also high, and China rapidly added its share. Asian countries responded to their crises by trying to further boost exports, in a cut-throat competition with one another. Korea's export volumes rose by 30 per cent during the first six months of 1998 (FEER 1998c). Low-cost Asian imports flooded world markets and pulled down prices worldwide, depressing earnings growth and reducing profit rates still further. The IMF restructuring plans were designed to slash this excess capacity by slowing borrowing and spending in the Asian economies. Recessions began to eliminate the weakest firms, leaving the market to the strongest, most efficient firms. The human costs of such an approach, however, were high. The International Labor Organization (ILO) predicted that over 10 million jobs would be lost region-wide as a result of the crisis.

The IMF reform programs produced conditions that benefitted many US firms. As weakened Asian currencies drove down prices, and as desperate governments invited foreigners into their economies, US companies bought up their Asian competitors. A former chief economist at Merrill Lynch & Co said: 'People with the longest time horizon and the deepest pockets are being given a once-in-a-generation opportunity' (*LA Times* 1998). US companies gained access to long protected markets. Foreign lenders pressured Asian governments to open areas such as finance and telecommunications that were traditionally protected from foreign ownership. In addition, US corporations obtained distribution networks and expanded low-cost manufacturing operations at 'rock-bottom' prices. Foreign investment in Korea during the first half of 1998 jumped by 30 per cent over the previous year. General Electric, for example, went on a 'buying spree' (*LA Times* 1998). Other US companies, such as Procter and Gamble and Hewlett-Packard, also bought into Korea's domestic market by absorbing troubled local firms.

At about the same time, the US Federal Reserve brokered a bailout of a major US speculative investment firm in order to prevent large losses for major US banks, to prop up falling US stock market prices and to forestall a credit crunch. Chairman Alan Greenspan said the intervention was necessary to avoid a 'fire sale' of US assets that might trigger a slowdown of the US economy in 1999 (AP 1998). Asian observers were troubled by the apparent double standard at work among US policy makers. At the 1998 IMF meetings, they sharply criticized the Fund (and the US Treasury, widely viewed as the power behind the Fund) for being insensitive to the political turmoil and human misery that the IMF policies entailed for Asia (*New York Times*, 1998), while the same agencies protected US business interests. Reports from Asia confirmed that bitterness and desperation, ' ... there is a perception of double standards and even racism' (*FEER* 1998d), had reached the point where isolationist and anti-Western solutions rose to the top of the agenda.

In mid-1998, Thailand, South Korea and Malaysia broke with the original IMF plans and began to expand their domestic economies by making lower interest rate funds available to their at-risk domestic businesses. The spread of financial crises around the globe to Russia and Latin America pressured the IMF to accede to the domestic interest rate cuts. Malaysia, which had never agreed to the initial IMF programs, established currency and capital flow controls that reduced speculation and allowed Malaysian policy makers to reflate their economy without triggering additional destructive capital outflows. The Malaysians explicitly compared their steps to those employed by the Japanese in the 1950s and early 1960s and to those employed by China and Taiwan more recently (*FEER* 1998e). They claimed that their actions represented the right of Asian economies to be managed in their populations' interest, instead of for the benefit of Western corporations and governments.

Joseph Stiglitz contends that IMF policy represents a 'Washington Consensus' that good economic development performance requires liberalized trade and financial systems, macroeconomic stability with the stress on low rates of inflation, and 'getting prices right' by increasing reliance on the market through financial deregulation and privatization. In other words, the 'consensus' is that the IMF should serve as the lead agency in a concerted effort to get Asian governments 'out of the way' so that private markets can more efficiently regulate and guide economic activity along the best path to increased growth and improved welfare in the region. In the context of the Asian crisis, Stiglitz questions the wisdom of this Washington consensus. He argues that its efforts can not produce economic development success because development also requires sound financial regulation, competition policy, transfer of technology and access to international markets as well as policies to support sustainable, egalitarian and democratic development policies (Stiglitz 1998a). We believe that the capitalist development lessons learned earlier by East Asian policy makers are not likely to be forgotten simply because they are now encountering structural adjustments imposed by the IMF. More egalitarian development with a greater amount of security than is common in the institutional arrangements of Western capitalism will most probably continue in East Asia, despite the late 1990s financial disasters. Malaysia's open rebellion against, and Japan's quiet resistance to, IMF imperatives are simply the first signs of a likely counter-attack.

Lessons learned: aid policy successes

Historically, aid to Pacific Rim countries first came from large US grants during the 1940s, 1950s and 1960s to build anticommunist alliances. This aid supplemented aggressive land reform programs with valuable inputs (seeds, fertilizers, pesticides, equipment, etc.), funded major physical and human infrastructure development and jump-started industrialization efforts. The second round of aid, during the late 1960s through the early 1980s, consisted of increased access to US markets and of transfers of technology facilitated by institutional support from US mass marketing companies and, especially, Japanese trading and manufacturing companies. Increased Japanese aid was funded by their enormous domestic savings and trade surpluses during those decades and motivated by the planned reorganization of their global production system. The most recent round of aid, billed as emergency funding intended to mitigate the Asian financial crisis of the late 1990s, consisted completely of loans brokered by the IMF. This aid was made conditional on enactment by the recipient countries on the Pacific Rim of politically inspired economic policy changes. The required IMF policy changes threatened to undermine and perhaps even destroy the East Asian 'growth-with-equity' model. The Asian financial crisis has made it possible for global financial capitalists to move toward eliminating the troublesome social costs and government restrictions associated with the East Asian model. The imposition of the IMF reforms also threatened the socioeconomic foundations of East Asian development success by ignoring the lessons of that success.

The US role in the Asian economic crisis was seen differently by the United States than it was by Asian countries. Clinton administration policy makers employed the IMF to carry out US aid policy towards Asia. The IMF acted aggressively to impose free-market, structural adjustment focused solutions to Asian financial problems. Forceful support of the IMF efforts by Treasury Secretary Rubin and Chief Economist Yellen attempted to disarm the troublesome Republican dominated US Congress whose growing isolationism threatened global capitalists' efforts to promote continued expansion of international production and markets (Weisberg 1998: 8–10). On the other hand, the high costs imposed on Asia by the international financial community's mistakes, and by the conditions the IMF tied to its bailouts, are being borne by the ordinary citizens of those countries. When the Asian economies recover, as they most likely will, Asian policy makers will have relearned, perhaps even more certainly than before, lessons about the continued importance of independent political control over their economic policy and the limited value of recent US advice for maintaining the soundness of their economic systems.

In the context of the debates over the causes and consequences of the Asian financial crisis, a struggle over policy approaches has developed within the IMF and the World Bank. Joseph Stiglitz, the chief economist at the World Bank, proposed a post-'Washington Consensus' model that challenged the structural adjustment, free-market policies that the IMF has promoted for the past two decades and which it has imposed in Asia during the 1990s crisis. Stiglitz' (1998a) focus was on the importance of sound financial regulation, sound competition policies, transfer of technology and access to international markets. This regulatory framework requires social policies which support sustainable, egalitarian and democratic development. Stiglitz' position was an explicit nod towards the continued viability and essential role of the historic East Asian model. In particular, his contribution should be recognized as one of a growing number that have re-emphasized the essential role that careful state regulation of economic development, attention to institution building, redistributive policies and facilitation of access to international markets played to promote shared, beneficial economic and social development.

Our book has shown in the cases of Taiwan, Korea and Costa Rica that when the rewards of growth were shared by a large segment of the population additional growth was encouraged. In Taiwan and South Korea, the foundations for a more egalitarian distribution of the benefits of growth were established by thoroughgoing land reform. In Costa Rica, the social-democratic policies that redistributed income and promoted social consumption served the same function. Expenditures on human development, including large expenditures on education and preventative health care, were important in all three of the successful development aid models analyzed in this book. In Korea and Taiwan, governments supported education and also agricultural cooperatives which invested heavily in advanced technologies, allowing farm families to direct more of their surplus toward education for their children. In Costa Rica, social-democratic governments spent a great deal on socialized health and education. All three countries, despite their acceptance of and dependence upon aid, did not defer to external agencies on important decisions. They also did not rely totally on unregulated markets. Instead, strong government bureaucracies committed to local development goals diligently planned and regulated economic development. For example, each government protected newly established domestic industries until they could compete internationally, despite US pressures to permit unfettered imports. Finally, government officials challenged USAID bureaucrats who tried to impose culturally or ideologically inappropriate decisions.

The concluding lesson from the history of successful US aid is that, although necessary, grant aid to build infrastructure, transfer technology and provide essential, but costly imports was not sufficient to assure development in Taiwan, South Korea or Costa Rica. Neither were their well-administered, domestically oriented development plans sufficient. Access to the massive US consumer market was the final element that promoted these countries' development. Their tremendous export growth would not have been possible without the special market access provided to these 'close allies' by US government assistance. Favorable tariff exemptions and quotas were combined with direct contacts with US buyers to spur the manufacture of products specifically targeted to US customers. In addition, the US government encouraged the establishment of a Pacific Rim division of labor in which Japanese trading companies and manufacturers linked Taiwan and Korea into the Japanese production and marketing network aimed at the US. These factors allowed these countries to pursue and achieve relatively independent economic development that benefitted their populations rather than solely outside economic interests.

Taiwan and China: surviving the Asian crisis

Taiwan was among the countries least affected by the Asian financial crisis. We believe that their continued stability, in contrast to South Korea's susceptibility to crisis, was a consequence of Taiwan's continued adherence to the lessons they learned while achieving relatively independent economic development. In 1997, Taiwan's real GNP growth was almost 7 per cent, private fixed investment increased by over 15 per cent, the unemployment rate was under 3 per cent and the inflation rate was less than 1 per cent (Kuo and Liu 1998: 58). Taiwan's stock market prices remained relatively stable from mid-June 1997 to the end of March 1998 and its currency decline (about 15 per cent) was less than half that experienced by other Asian nations. Taiwan's trade account registered a surplus every year from 1990 to 1997 averaging about 4 per cent of GDP. The surpluses helped domestic savings exceed investment. Consequently, Taiwan's foreign debt fell while other Asian countries' debt rose.

The Taiwan government designed a package of economic and financial measures during the 1990s to prevent an excess inflow of (speculative) foreign investment. They used new investment to upgrade the technology content of their industries as they redirected investments in traditional industries to low unit labor cost, and hence internationally competitive, sites in mainland China. 'The Hsinchu Science-based Industrial Park ... became a powerful driving force for advancement and growth in the manufacturing sector. Taiwan became the world's third-largest producer of information products in 1995' (ibid.: 63). From 1981 to 1996, the share of technology-intensive industries (e.g., electrical and electronic equipment, precision machinery, vehicles) in domestic industry increased from 20 to 38 per cent, while the share of traditional industries (e.g., food processing, clothing, textiles, footwear) fell from 43 per cent to 27 per cent (ibid.: 76). Meanwhile, high-tech exports increased their share of total exports from 24 to 38 per cent from 1989 to 1996, while low-tech exports share fell from 38 to 21 per cent (ibid.: 77). Intermediate products exports rose from 40 to 57 per cent of the total as Taiwanese firms exported increasingly sophisticated products to support their offshore production of traditional goods in mainland China. Taiwan's trade surplus with mainland China amounted to over 220 per cent of its global trade surplus in 1997 (Lin 1998: 86). By 1977, over 60 per cent of its foreign investment, which totaled US$21 billion, went to the mainland (ibid.: 87).

Taiwanese venture capitalist firms provided funds, researched technology, developed manufacturing processes, drafted business plans and recruited skilled employees for the new domestic firms in which they invested during the late 1990s (*FEER* 1998f). The government steered these venture capital investments into high-technology industries with investment tax credits, tax rebates and with relaxed regulations that permitted the high-technology startup firms to go public more easily than other companies. Consequently, electronics companies tripled their share of capitalization in Taiwan's stock market in the five years between 1993 and 1998 (*FEER* 1998f). Both the electronics and bio-tech startups found homes in the government-established Hsinchu Science Park. These investors also took advantage of their connections with US markets in the Silicon Valley and other high-tech regions. As a result, from 1981 to 1997 trade grew at an annual rate close to 30 per cent. Taiwan's yearly trade surplus reached US$18 billion in 1997 (Lin 1998: 86).

In order to build up and stabilize domestic demand, the Taiwan government made infrastructural construction projects an increasingly important part of its development plans from 1986 to 1996. Public investment as a share of GDP rose substantially (Kuo and Liu 1998: 64–5). Public foreign debt was virtually zero and the foreign assets of the private sector exceeded its debt (ibid.: 68). Foreign investment in domestic companies was restricted to substantially less than half (ibid.: 68). The net effect of these conditions was that, although foreign capital came into Taiwan during the 1990s, most of it was directed into productive investments that upgraded Taiwan's industrial structure. On the other hand, Taiwanese firms' foreign investments expanded their capacity to continue to effectively compete in ever more difficult export markets. Coupled with increased government investment, Taiwan's domestic capacity to consume rose and encouraged domestically oriented growth as well.

China also followed a cautiously planned and carefully regulated integration into the international economy. In 1996, China introduced currency convertibility for importers and exporters to facilitate foreign trade, but it retained control over capital flows, especially over potentially volatile short-term flows. Therefore, like Taiwan, China was sheltered from speculative capital inflows and unrestrained growth of short-term foreign debt. Consequently, China was also sheltered from the worst effects of the Asian crisis. China's GDP growth for the first six months of 1998 was at a 7 per cent annual rate, down from 9 per cent in 1997. Exports grew at 7.5 per cent for the first six months, down from 26 per cent during the comparable period in 1997 (China News Digest 1998). China responded to slowed export growth by increasing its domestic spending on infrastructure to try to avoid slipping into recession.

In August 1998, Chinese economists urged their government to avoid competitive currency devaluations that might provoke destructive retaliations from their crisis-threatened competitors. Instead, they proposed that China's trade surplus be maintained by import restrictions on consumer goods. These economists also urged continued restrictions on capital inflows and outflows in order to dampen any speculation against the Chinese currency. In late 1998, Chinese authorities tightened their administration of the current account (i.e., trade) rules in order to close loopholes that allowed some illegal capital flows. These changes were considered to be especially important because, although China's foreign exchange reserves increased by US$40 billion to US$140 billion from the end of 1996 to the beginning of 1998, the reserves had leveled out as Chinese export growth slowed due to the trade dampening effects of the Asian crisis. In other words, China made explicit efforts to avoid the mistakes that had left South Korea's economy open to the spreading Asian financial crisis.

Lessons learned: aid policy failures

The United States Agency for International Development failed to promote development in the countries over which it had the most significant political-economic influence. US aid monies were squandered in Vietnam in the 1950s and 1960s, in El Salvador in the 1980s and in Nicaragua in the early 1990s on programs which did not produce growth with equity. In these countries, the US supported elite classes who appropriated aid for their own purposes rather than spend it to implement progressive developmental programs. When there was a clear political alternative to the US-dominated elite, such as a national liberation movement or socialist party, then bilateral aid ended up causing, or greatly aggravating, civil conflict in these countries. Whether the political alternative was present in another region of the country, as in North Vietnam; or in the guerrilla or liberated zones, as in Vietnam and El Salvador; or in the legislature, as in 1990s Nicaragua, US aid boosted the capacity of anti-popular elites to attack their challengers.

US support for elite groups that were increasingly separated from and hostile to their domestic population created a particularly insidious form of foreign aid dependence. When foreign aid personnel from the US-developed and -administered programs in small countries and when that aid determined domestic policy, the national purpose and identity of the recipient countries was subverted. We have described how USAID policies both corrupted and crippled Vietnamese 'counterpart' bureaucrats in Vietnam so that they were unable to make real political or economic decisions. USAID policies did not allow the Vietnamese to develop necessary, culturally and economically appropriate development-supporting institutions. The Vietnamese were forced to attempt to replicate market capitalism in their country without the necessary institutional foundations that were developed in Taiwan and South Korea. In this environment of dependence and domination, the political and economic results were disastrous for the Vietnamese people.

USAID domination of national decision making in Central America also prevented successful development. Though aid programs in El Salvador and Nicaragua were implemented differently than they were in Vietnam, the failure to truly assist the majority of the population was similar. USAID deserted, and often subverted, Central American leaders who did not line up with US ideological demands and who did not enthusiastically support free-market 'reforms.' USAID sought out and supplied right-wing groups and individuals who then destabilized the political center in El Salvador and who attacked the official government in Nicaragua. Aid funds enabled these right-wing organizations to buy political support in the military and in the countryside. Despite this significant economic and military aid, however, USAID was unable to advance development in these countries in which it had the most significant political-economic influence. Cold War USAID officials never understood the indigenous situation well enough for their policies to have their intended results. Reforms followed reforms in the subjugated countries but the 'hearts and minds' of the native peoples were not won over. In an environment of dependence and domination, development of institutions that would allow local control and local benefit did not occur. Aid was effective in influencing elections, in promoting cronyism and, ultimately, in advancing large-scale immigration of Southeast Asians and Central Americans to the US. Aid was not successful in promoting growth in Vietnam (either before or after the resumption of hostilities in the 1960s) in El Salvador in the 1980s or Nicaragua after the electoral defeat of the Sandinistas.

In retrospect, it is clear that the programs that most effectively promoted popular development, like the 1980 land reform in El Salvador and the 1970 land reform in Vietnam, were the programs whose content and effects were most closely aligned with the programs supported by the anti-elite social forces that had faced the brunt of US attacks and subversion. In Central America, the foreign policy of the Clinton administration has perceptibly shifted the direction and effects of aid policies. After so many years of divisive class politics supportive of anti-democratic elites, support for the popular development aspects of the peace agreements in El Salvador and Guatemala was a step in the right direction. Unfortunately, the old elites and right-wing politicians, for the time being, still maintain their power and still block development with equity.

Overall economic impacts of postwar aid

Postwar US aid commitments to East and Southeast Asia were extraordinary in their sheer size as well as their political and economic impacts. From the serious mistakes in US aid policy in some cases and the extraordinary and unexpected positive economic growth results in others, we have learned valuable lessons about the possibilities and limits of foreign aid.

The vast amount, over $20 billion, of US aid to Vietnam was concentrated in a twenty-year period between 1955 and 1975 and, as we have seen, was in large part wasted. Aid to Taiwan was very significant, especially on a per capita basis, but during most of the aid period, the years after 1961, this economic aid consisted mainly of loans rather than grants. Nevertheless, by that time Taiwanese development was well under way and grants were not needed. The largest amount of United States grants in aid, in the postwar period, went to South Korea. Even on a per capita basis Korea received the largest amount of grant aid. US aid continued to flow to Korea in the 1960s and 1970s, and even up to the mid-1980s. The import-

Table 8.1 US grants and credits to selected east and southeast asian countries US$ billions (1987)

	Philippines	S. Korea	S. Vietnam	Taiwan
Grants/Credits	10.6	25.8	21.4	13.9
	(1945–90)	(1945–85)	(1954–75)	(1945–82)
Population	61 mil.	40 mil.	19 mil.	20 mil.
	(1990)	(1990)	(1975)	(1990)

Source: US Bureau of Economic Analysis. See Appendix 1.

ance of this aid has largely been underplayed in explanations of Korean development (for example in Amsden, 1989). In both Korea and Taiwan, as we showed in Chapters 3 and 4, aid effectively supported growth with equity. In contrast to this highly favorable historical treatment, post-Cold War financial aid to South Korea has been limited to the recent loans during the Asian financial crisis, which have come with many strings attached.

Most US foreign aid programs have had less significant impacts for good or ill than the clear successes and failures we have analyzed in this book. For example, the smaller amounts of aid the Philippines received (half as much post-WWII aid as South Korea, even less on a per capita basis) seem only enough to have satisfied the corrupt appetites of the political elites receiving the funds. Aid funds were sufficient to insure their political allegiance, but not enough in the right kinds of programs to make a significant, positive development impact. Even more importantly, as we explained in Chapter 2, these elites were maintained in power because redistributive New Deal programs like land reform were not supported in the Philippines, as they were in Taiwan and South Korea in the 1950s. The failure to positively alter the unequal distribution of resources and political power in the Philippines blocked beneficial development.

Conclusion: aid in the future

As we enter the new millennium, the world is more politically and economically interconnected. The effects of the Asian financial crisis have spread around the globe – to Russia, Latin America, Europe and, finally, to the United States. According to Ryrie (1995), there are three different motivations for aid: humanitarian, commercial and political. In this context, US interests in Pacific Rim development were predominantly political – fighting communism – and Japanese interests have been largely commercial – the establishment of East Asian trade networks. With their very different motivations, these two countries helped to demonstrate that international cooperation and market development can work for real improvement in living standards for a very large segment of the world's poorer countries. Will the United States, absent Cold War political and ideological motivations, be interested in supporting future projects for economic improvement in other countries? Or will the US continue, through the IMF and other international agencies, to push free-market structural adjustment policies that cripple the recipient economies? In our interconnected world, it would seem to be in the long-run interest of the already developed countries to assist their trading partners in the development of strong, growing and stable economies. The newly emerging economies of the last 30 years proved that capitalist development with shared benefits was possible in a few poor countries in East Asia and Central America. Effective aid programs could be modelled on East Asia's experience to make such development widespread. Unfortunately, it is equally possible that, without the fear of communism on the horizon, capitalist countries will only provide aid in the event of financial emergencies – and then only as a pretext to open them up to unregulated and destabilizing trade and investment.

If, in the future, altruistic motivations or fear of poverty and instability cause policy makers from developed countries to extend substantial grants in aid to LDCs, then we have shown that such aid can promote sustainable growth with equity if it is deployed in the appropriate institutional settings. We have also shown that, while the 'free-market' model may meet the needs of international firms, it does not promote development with equity by itself. Effective aid programs are those that promote access to developed country markets, including building concrete links between producers in LDCs and marketers in the developed world. In order to realize the benefits of aid, it must be used to construct institutions that facilitate broad-based sharing of the fruits of development, because the expansion of markets without improving people's lives is simply exploitation and not development. Lastly, aid means help, not outside political control. Without strong indigenous leadership, aid efforts are bound to repeat the failures of US aid in the Cold War period.

Appendix 1

US FOREIGN GRANTS AND CREDITS TO FAR EAST IN MILLION $
REAL VALUES, 1987 = 100

Year	Japan	S. Korea	Philippines	Taiwan	Vietnam	Far East	Deflator
1945	15	8	218	910	0	1338	13.3
1946	2198	198	251	1886	0	4982	16.7
1947	2508	449	802	1000	0	4888	18.7
1948	1860	670	665	755	0	4285	20.0
1949	2618	387	1020	166	0	4533	19.9
1950	1119	505	990	89	0	3010	20.2
1951	1131	554	61	305	0	2376	21.3
1952	167	721	47	372	0	1781	21.5
1953	−14	936	109	409	0	1805	22.0
1954	32	761	41	401	185	1757	22.2
1955	284	1218	92	476	886	3424	22.9
1956	521	1275	119	475	970	4254	23.6
1957	193	1283	160	402	967	4004	24.4
1958	−24	1249	169	337	876	3153	24.9
1959	188	906	94	336	691	2797	25.6
1960	69	1004	92	419	715	3023	26.0
1961	99	875	46	452	574	2844	26.3
1962	213	888	97	306	586	2892	26.8
1963	118	882	40	279	779	2853	27.2
1964	177	570	177	162	798	2069	27.7
1965	−201	588	162	173	1060	2282	28.4
1966	160	571	75	102	1711	3313	29.4
1967	−30	637	109	125	1323	3304	30.3
1968	−390	601	107	101	1374	3248	31.8
1969	66	778	87	36	1335	3425	33.4
1970	−153	563	179	40	1188	2798	35.2
1971	−208	612	174	44	1347	3098	31.7
1972	−154	568	180	67	1386	3129	38.9
1973	−557	518	172	94	1061	2295	41.3
1974	4	140	96	265	1303	3051	44.9
1975	20	638	157	388	337	2360	49.2
1976	111	658	208	277	0	2067	52.3
1977	−86	447	270	123	0	1288	55.9
1978	76	1158	199	86	0	2056	60.3
1979	−105	348	215	261	0	1483	65.6
1980	−68	141	46	541	0	1163	71.7
1981	86	380	74	242	0	1181	78.9
1982	−100	567	74	41	0	970	83.8
1983	−18	514	276	−50	0	1370	87.2
1984	−109	228	155	−158	0	722	91.1
1985	−92	61	354	−270	0	233	94.4
1986	−91	−151	463	−270	0	−66	96.9
1987	−319	−1717	331	−970	0	−2614	100.0
1988	−4	−369	405	−8	0	296	103.9
1989	−1	−122	286	−6	0	351	108.4
1990	−562	−170	493	−6	0	−117	112.9

Data from US Dept. of Commerce *Historical Statistics of the US* (to 1970) and *Statistical Abstracts of the US* (1945–1992)

Appendix 2

US FOREIGN GRANTS AND CREDITS TO CENTRAL AMERICA IN MILLION $
REAL VALUES, 1987 = 100

Year	Costa Rica	El Salvador	Honduras	Guatemala	Nicaragua	C. America	S&C. America	Deflator
1945	8	8	0	0	0	15	75	13.3
1946	12	0	0	12	6	30	503	16.7
1947	0	0	0	5	11	16	594	18.7
1948	0	0	0	10	0	10	290	20.0
1949	0	0	0	10	0	10	367	19.9
1950	0	0	0	5	0	5	317	20.2
1951	5	0	0	0	0	5	535	21.3
1952	9	0	5	5	5	23	423	21.5
1953	9	5	5	0	5	23	1705	22.0
1954	9	5	5	0	5	23	306	22.2
1955	22	4	9	48	9	92	445	22.9
1956	13	4	8	85	8	119	640	23.6
1957	37	4	12	94	12	160	1037	24.4
1958	40	4	20	48	20	133	2281	24.9
1959	31	4	23	35	16	109	1320	25.6
1960	15	4	15	62	31	127	746	26.0
1961	27	30	30	53	34	175	2703	26.3
1962	34	22	15	34	26	131	2190	26.8
1963	26	40	18	37	26	147	2118	27.2
1964	36	36	14	32	25	144	1617	27.7
1965	49	39	35	39	25	187	2268	28.4
1966	34	58	24	27	37	180	2514	29.4
1967	40	36	20	50	30	175	2162	30.3
1968	35	22	22	53	31	164	2535	31.8
1969	39	21	27	30	51	168	1811	33.4
1970	23	28	28	28	60	168	1537	35.2
1971	32	22	25	35	41	155	1284	31.7
1972	28	23	26	44	15	136	1185	38.9
1973	24	22	24	36	48	155	1283	41.3
1974	20	9	29	38	40	136	1780	44.9
1975	20	14	49	43	26	152	1679	49.2
1976	13	17	34	82	33	180	1197	52.3
1977	9	25	32	43	38	147	984	55.9
1978	12	18	27	27	41	124	1275	60.3
1979	12	15	43	26	44	140	1265	65.6
1980	4	68	28	21	109	230	1649	71.7
1981	14	153	57	23	19	266	745	78.9
1982	55	286	101	27	7	477	2209	83.8
1983	232	374	128	38	3	775	936	87.2
1984	201	490	231	27	1	950	2280	91.1
1985	226	475	257	55	-2	1011	2269	94.4
1986	143	388	231	94	0	857	1889	96.9
1987	159	417	212	159	0	947	2100	100.0
1988	103	390	187	137	0	816	1394	103.9
1989	132	375	123	149	0	778	1030	108.4
1990	91	266	193	81	86	717	1671	112.9

Data from US Dept. of Commerce Historical Statistics of the US (to 1970) and Statistical Abstracts of the US (1945–1992)

Appendix 3

EXPORTS FROM CENTRAL AMERICA TO THE US IN MILLION $

Year	Guatemala	Honduras	El Salvador	Nicaragua	Costa Rica	TOTAL
1980	426	392	214	160	360	1552
1981	294	346	102	135	329	1206
1982	296	364	108	98	295	1160
1983	407	371	286	157	297	1519
1984	419	342	215	49	358	1382
1985	359	342	217	71	378	1367
1986	490	390	352	21	467	1720
1987	346	428	267	0	500	1542
1988	368	268	224	0	494	1354
1989	392	498	178	0	534	1602
1990	463	*415*	139	0	*654*	1672
1991	455	331	128	52	775	1740
1992	459	390	186	60	880	1975
1993	511	379	213	115	872	2089
1994	483	330	183	149	963	2109
1995	606	279	*153*	209	1198	2445

Italics indicate estimated data

Data from United Nations *1980–1996 International Trade Statistics Yearbooks: Trade by Country*

Bibliography

Agency for International Development. 1991. *Economic Assistance Strategy for Central America 1991–2000*. Washington DC: Agency for International Development.

Alam, M. Shahid. 1989. *Governments and Markets in Economic Development Strategies*. New York: Praeger.

Amin, Samir. 1976. *Unequal Development: An Essay on the Social Formations of Peripheral Capitalism*. New York: Monthly Review Press.

Amsden, Alice H. 1979. 'Taiwan's Economic History', *Modern China*, 5 (3): 341–80.

Amsden, Alice H. 1985. 'The State and Taiwan's Economic Development', in P. Evans, D. Rueschemeyer and T. Skocpal (eds), *Bringing the State Back In*. Cambridge: Cambridge University Press.

Amsden, Alice H. 1989. *Asia's Next Giant*. Oxford: Oxford University Press.

Amsden, Alice H. 1991a. 'Diffusion of Development: The Late Industrializing Model and Greater East Asia', *American Economic Review*, 81 (2): 282–6.

Amsden, Alice H. 1991b. 'Big Business and Urban Congestion in Taiwan', *World Development*, 19 (9): 1121–35.

Amsden, Alice H. 1992. 'Taiwan in International Perspective', in N.T. Wang (ed.), *Taiwan's Enterprises in Global Perspective*.

Amsden, Alice H. 1994. 'Why Isn't the Whole World Experimenting with the East Asian Model to Develop?', Review of *The East Asian Miracle*, *World Development*, 22 (4): 627–33.

Amsden, Alice H. and Takashi Hikino. 1993. 'Borrowing Technology or Innovating: An Exploration of the Two Paths to Industrial Development', in Ross Thompson (ed.), *Learning and Technological Change*, New York: Macmillan.

AP. 1998. Associated Press report, 2 October.

Archard, Douglas B. 1971. Letter to Richard Eney, Director, Land Reform Division, Military Region IV, 19 October.

Armstrong, Robert and Shenk, Janet. 1982. *El Salvador: The Face of Revolution*. Boston: South End Press.

Arrigo, Linda Gail. 1993. 'A Brief Report on Taiwan's Legislative Yuan Elections', *Bulletin of Concerned Asian Scholars*, 25 (1): 34–40.

Balassa, Bela. 1981. *Development Strategies in Semi-Industrial Economies*. Washington DC: World Bank.

Balassa, Bela. 1988. 'The Lessons of East Asian Development', *Economic Development and Cultural Change*, 36 (3): 5273–90.

Balassa, Bela. 1991. *Economic Policies in the Pacific Area Developing Countries*. New York: NYU Press.

Ballantyne, Janet. 1992. 'The United States Version', *Barricada International*, 12 (353): 13–14.

Ban, Sung-Hwan, Pal Yong Moon and Dwight Perkins. 1980. *Rural Development*. Cambridge, MA: Harvard University Press.

Baran, Paul. 1957. *The Political Economy of Growth*. New York: Monthly Review Press.

Barricada International. 1997. 'Aleman Backs Down', 17 (401): 4–6.

Barry, Tom. 1987. *Roots of Rebellion: Land and Hungry in Central America*. Boston: South End Press.

Behrman, Jere R. 1993. *Human Resource Led Development? Review of Issues and Evidence*. Geneva: International Labour Office.

Bello, Walden and Stephanie Rosenfeld. 1990. *Dragons in Distress*. San Francisco: Food First.

Bendaña, Alejandro. 1991. *Una Tañgedia Campesina: Tesimonios de la Resistencia*. Managua: Editora de Arte.

Bernstein, Henry. 1982. 'Industrialization, Development, and Dependence', in Hamza Alavi and Teodor Shanin (eds), *Introduction to the Sociology of Developing Societies*. New York: Monthly Review Press.

Birdsall, Nancy. 1992. 'Social Development is Economic Development'. Presentation to Delegates of the Social Committee, United Nations General Assembly, New York: 19 October.

Borge, Tomás. 1992. 'Aid That Isn't', *Barricada International*, 12 (353): 10–11.

Borthwick, Mark. 1992. *Pacific Century: The Emergence of Modern Pacific Asia*. Boulder: Westview and Allen & Unwin.

Boyce, James K. (ed.). 1996. *Economic Policy for Building Peace*. Boulder and London: Lynne Rienner Publishers.

Boyce, James K. 1995. 'External Assistance and the Peace Process in El Salvador', *World Development*, 23 (12): 2101–16.

Branigan, William.1987. 'Nicaraguan Rebels' Tactics Assailed', *The Washington Post*, 17 May, A28–9.

Bredo, William, Robert O. Shreve and William J. Tater. 1968. *Land Reform in Vietnam: Working Papers*, vol. III. Menlo Park, CA: Stanford Research Institute.

Burris, Val. 1992. 'Late Industrialization and Class Formation in East Asia'. *Research in Political Economy*. 13: 245–83.

Byrne, Hugh. 1996. *El Salvador's Civil War: A Study of Revolution*. Boulder and London: Lynne Rienner Publishers.

Callison, C. Stuart. 1972. 'The Economic, Social and Political Effects of the Land to the Tiller Program'. Progress Report on Dissertation. Yale University (mimeo).

Cassen, Robert and Associates. 1994. *Does Aid Work?*, 2nd edn. Oxford: Clarendon Press.

Chang, C.C. 1992. 'The Development of Taiwan's Personal Computer Industry'. in N.T. Wang. (ed.), *Taiwan's Enterprises in Global Perspective*.

Chang, C.P. 1998. 'ROC Economic Development'. *Industry of Free China*, January.

Chang, Ha-Joon. 1997. 'Perspective on Korea', *LA Times*, 31 December.

Chen, C.N. 1992. 'Internationalization of Taiwan's Toy Industry', in N.T. Wang (ed.), *Taiwan's Enterprises in Global Perspective*.

Child, Frank C. 1962. *Toward a Policy of Economic Growth in Vietnam.* East Lansing, Michigan: Michigan State Advisory Group.

China News Digest. 1998. International news, www.cnd.org. 21 October.

Cho, Dong-Sung. 1987. *The General Trading Company.* Lexington, MA: D.C. Heath.

Choussudosky, Michel. 1997. 'The IMF Korea Bailout'. e-mail publication from chosso@travel-net.com. December.

Christian, Shirley. 1986. *Nicaragua: Revolution in the Family.* New York: Random House.

Cohen, Theodore 1987. *Remaking Japan: The American Occupation as New Deal.* New York: Free Press.

Cole, David C. and Princeton N. Lyman. 1971. *Korean Development: The Interplay of Politics and Economics.* Cambridge, MA: Harvard University Press.

Collins, Joseph, Lappe, Frances Moore and Allen, Nick 1985. *What Difference Could a Revolution Make?* San Francisco: Food First.

Congressional Quarterly Service. 1965. Congress and the Nation: 1945–1964. Washington, DC: Government Printing Office.

Counsel for Economic Planning and Development (CEPD). 1993. *An Initiative into the Next Century.* Taipei: CEPD.

Cumings, Bruce. 1984. 'The Origins and Development of the Northeast Asian Political Economy', *International Organization,* 38 (1): 1–40.

Daly, Rex, Hoffman, Robert, Nelson, Frederick, Weingarten, Hyman and Hancock (Wiegersma), Nancy *et al.* 1973. *Agriculture in Vietnam's Economy.* Washington DC: US Department of Agriculture, International Development Center.

D'Costa, Anthony P. 1994. 'State, Steel and Strength: Structural Competitiveness and Development in South Korea', *Journal of Development Studies,* 31 (1): 44–81.

Deere, Carmen Diana and Diskin, Martin. 1983. 'Rural Poverty in El Salvador: Dimensions, Trends and Causes'. Geneva: International Labour Office.

Deere, Carmen Diana, Marchetti, Peter and Reinhardt, Nola. 1985. 'The Peasantry and the Development of Sandinista Agrarian Policy', *Latin American Research Review,* 20 (3): 75–109.

Deighton, Jane, Horsley, Rosanna, Stewart, Sarah and Cain, Cathy. 1983. *Sweet Ramparts: Women in Revolutionary Nicaragua.* London: War a Want/ Nicaraguan Solidarity Campaign.

Eberstadt, Nick. 1985. 'The Perversion of Foreign Aid: America's Failed Economic and Military Aid', *Commentary,* 79: 21.

Economic Survey Mission to Vietnam. 1956. *Toward the Economic Development of the Republic of Vietnam.* Rome: United Nations.

Economist, The. 1997. 'New illness, same old medicine.' December 13: 65–6.

Ellis, Keneth. 1988. Rural Development Officer, USAID, San Salvador, El Salvador, interview with Nan Wiegersma and Nola Reinhardt, 10 July.

Envio. 1991a. 'Economic Stabilization- Stop Inflation, and Then What?', 10 (121): 13–22.

Envio. 1991b. 'How to Get Foreign Aid: Making the Poor Pay Isn't Enough', 10 (118): 29–38.

Envio. 1991c. 'Property', 10 (121): 23–6.

Envio. 1991d. 'Soladarismo: Nueva Arma Contra Los Sindicatos', 10 (115): 12–20.

Envio. 1991e. 'The Right Wing's Third Try for Power', 10 (121): 3–12.

Envio. 1991f. 'Tras Los Ajustes Económicos:- Qué-Ajustes Politicos Exige USA?', 10 (115): 1–11.

Fall, Bernard B. 1964. *The Two Vietnams*, Rev. Edn. New York: Praeger.

Far Eastern Economic Review. 1998a. 'Money Isn't Everything', 12 February.

Far Eastern Economic Review. 1998b. 'Fund Under Fire', 14 May.

Far Eastern Economic Review. 1998c. Sender, Henny. 1 October.

Far Eastern Economic Review. 1998d. 'Losing Faith', 8 October.

Far Eastern Economic Review. 1998e. 'Desperate Measures', 10 September.

Far Eastern Economic Review. 1998f. 'Working Venture', 10 September.

Ferguson, William. 1991. 'Aid's Quiet War on Nicaragua', *Nicaragua Through Our Eyes* 6 (4): 1, 8.

Fitzgerald, E.V.K. 1986. 'Notes on the Analysis of the Small Underdeveloped Economy in Transition', in Fager *et al.* (eds), *Transition and Development*. New York: Monthly Review Press.

Fitzgerald, Frances. 1972. *Fire in the Lake*. New York: Random House.

Frank, Andre Gunder. 1967. *Capitalism and Underdevelopment in Latin America*. New York: Monthly Review Press.

Galenson, Walter (ed.). 1979. *Economic Growth and Structural Change in Taiwan*. Ithaca: Cornell University Press.

Gallin, Rita. 1990. 'Women and the Export Industry in Taiwan: the Muting of Class Consciousness', in Kathryn Ward (ed.), *Women Workers and Global Restructuring*. Ithaca, New York: ILR Press.

Garita, Luis. 1989. 'The Bureaucratization of the Costa Rican State', in Marc Ededman and Joanne Kenen (eds), *The Costa Rican Reader*. New York: Grove Weidenfeld.

Gittinger, Price. 1959. *Agrarian Reform in Free Vietnam*. Government Report, 15 September.

Gold, Thomas B. 1981. 'Dependent Development in Taiwan.' Ph.D. dissertation, Harvard University.

Gold, Thomas B. 1986. *State and Society in the Taiwan Miracle*. Armonk, NY: M.E. Sharpe.

Gold, Thomas B. 1988. 'Entrepreneurs, Multinationals, and the State', in Winckler and Greenhalgh (eds), *Contending Approaches to the Political Economy of Taiwan*.

Greenhalgh, Susan. 1988. 'Families and Networks in Taiwan's Economic Development', in Winckler and Greenhalgh (eds), *Contending Approaches to the Political Economy of Taiwan*.

Greenhalgh, Susan. 1988. 'Supranational Processes of Income Distribution', in Winckler and Greenhalgh (eds), *Contending Approaches to the Political Economy of Taiwan*.

Griffin, Keith. 1989. *Alternative Strategies for Economic Development*. London: Macmillan.

Gupta, Kanhaya, and Islam, M. Anisul. 1983. *Foreign Capital, Savings and Growth: An International Cross-Section Study*. Dordrecht, Holland and Boston: D. Reidel Publishing Co.

Guzman Stein, Laura. 1984. 'La industria de la maquila y la explotación de la fuerza de trabajo de la mujer', *Desarollo y Sociedad*, 12: 101–10.

Hall, Carolyn. 1985. *Costa Rica: A Geographical Interpretation in Historical Perspective*. Boulder and London: Westview Press.

Halliday, Jon. 1975. *A Political History of Japanese Capitalism*. New York: Pantheon Books.

Halliday, Jon and Gavan McCormack. 1973. *Japanese Imperialism Today*. New York: Monthly Review Press.

Hamilton, Clive. 1983. 'Capitalist Industrialization in East Asia's Four Little Tigers', *Journal of Contemporary Asia*, 13(1): 35–73.

Hanson, Harry (ed.). 1957. *The World Almanac, 1957*. New York: World Telegraph and Sun.

Harberger, Arnold C. 1993a. 'The Search for Relevance in Economics', *American Economic Review*, 83 (2): 1–16.

Harberger, Arnold C. 1993b. 'Secrets of Success', *American Economic Review*, 83 (2): 343–50.

Hart-Landsberg, Martin. 1979. 'Export-Led Industrialization in the Third World', *Review of Radical Political Economics*, 11 (4): 50–63.

Hart-Landsberg, Martin. 1991. 'The Asian NICs at the Crossroads', *Monthly Review*, 43 (4): 57–63.

Hart-Landsberg, Martin. 1993. *The Rush to Development*. New York: Monthly Review Press.

Hill, Richard. 1989. 'Divisions of Labor in Global Manufacturing', in Arthur MacEwen and William Tabb (eds), *Instability and Change in the World Economy*, New York: Monthly Review Press.

Ho, Au Ngoc. 1971. Minister of the Economy, 1968–9. Interview with Gareth Porter, September.

Ho, Samuel P.S. 1978. *Economic Development of Taiwan 1860–1970*. New Haven: Yale University Press.

Hobsbawm, Eric. 1992. 'The Crisis of Today's Ideologies', *New Left Review*, 192: 55–64.

Honey, Martha. 1994. *Hostile Acts: U.S. Policy in Costa Rica in the 1980s*. Gainesville: University Press of Florida.

Hsing, M.H. 1971. *Taiwan: Industrialization and Trade Policies*. Oxford: Oxford University Press.

International Monetary Fund. 1998a. *World Economic Outlook*, World Economic and Financial Surveys. Washington, DC: International Monetary Fund, May.

International Monetary Fund. 1998b. 'The IMF's Response to the Asian Crisis.' International Monetary Fund internet site, 15 June.

International Monetary Fund. 1998c. 'The Asian crisis and Implications for other Economies.' Address by Stanley Fischer delivered in Sao Paulo, Brazil. International Monetary Fund internet site, 19 June.

International Monetary Fund. 1998d. 'From the Asian Crisis to a New Global Architecture.' Address by Michel Camdessus delivered in Strasbourg, France. International Monetary Fund internet site, 23 June.

Irwan, Alexander. 1991. 'Contending Approaches to the Political Economy of Taiwan', *Journal of Contemporary Asia*, 21 (1): 115–18.

Jacoby, Neil H. 1966. *US Aid to Taiwan*. New York: Praeger.

Jiménez, Rudolfo and Victor Cespedes. 1990. 'Costa Rica: cambio estructural y situacíon social durante la crisis y la recuperacíon', in Claudia Gonzales Vega and editors, *Politicas Económicas en Costa Rica, Tomo II*. San José: Academia de Centroamérica.

Judis, John. 1993. 'World Bank', *In These Times*, 13 December: 14–15.

Ka, C.M. and Mark Selden, 1986. 'Original Accumulation, Equity and Late Industrialization', *World Development*, 14 (10/11): 1293–310.

Keane, John F. 1971. *Report on Land Reform and Politics in Go Cong*. District Senior Advisor, Hoa Tan District, Go Cong Province. US Agency for International Development.

Keesing, D.B. 1983. 'Linking Up to Distant Markets: South to North Exports of Manufactured Consumer Goods', *American Economic Review*, 3 (2): 338–42.

Kennedy, John Fitzgerald. 1973. 'Proposal for the Alliance for Progress', in Henry S. Commager (ed.), *Documents of American History, Volume II*. New Jersey: Prentice Hall.

Khaleque, Abdul. 1980. *Political Economy of Foreign Aid*. Daka: Polwel Printing Press.

Kim, Seung-Kyung. 1992. 'Women in the Labor Movement in South Korea' in Frances Rothsein and Michael Blim (eds), *Anthropology and the Global Factory*. New York: Bergin and Garvey.

Koo, Anthony Y.C. 1968. *The Role of Land Reform in Economic Development*. New York: Praeger.

Krueger, Anne O. 1990. 'Government Failures in Development', *Journal of Economic Perspectives*, 4 (3): 9–23.

Krueger, Anne O. 1997. 'Trade Policy and Economic Development: How We Learn', *American Economic Review*, 87(1): 1–22.

Krugman, Paul. 1993. 'The Narrow and Broad Arguments for Free Trade', *American Economic Review*, 83 (2): 362–6.

Kuo, Shirley W.Y. and Christina Y. Liu. 1998. 'Characteristics of the Taiwan Economy in the Context of the Asian Financial Crisis', *Industry of Free China*, July: 57–81.

Kuong, Nguyen Xuan. 1972. US AID employee and former director of the Cadaster, Vietnam. Interview with Nan Wiegersma (Hancock), April.

Kuznets, Paul W. 1988. 'An East Asian Model of Development', *Economic Development and Cultural Change*, 36 (3): 511–43.

LA Times. 1998. 'Asia's woes prove a capital opportunity', Evelyn Iritani 4 October.

Ladejinsky, Wolf Isaac. 1977. *Agrarian Reform as Unfinished Business: The Selected Papers of Wolf Ladejinksy*. London: Oxford University Press for the World Bank.

Ladejinsky, Wolf Isaac. 1955. 'Field Trip Observations in Central Vietnam.' Unpublished government document, 2 April.

Lal, Deepak and Sarath Rajapatirana. 1987. 'Foreign Trade Regimes and Economic Growth in Developing Countries', *The World Bank Research Observer*, 2 (2): 189–217.

Lall, Sanjaya. 1992. 'Technological Capabilities and Industrialization', *World Development*, 20 (2): 165–86.

Lall, Sanjaya. 1994. 'The East Asian Miracle: Does the Bell Toll for Industrial Strategy?', *World Development*, 22 (4): 645–54.

Landes, David and Flynn, Patricia. 1984. 'Dollars for Dictators', in Roger Burbach and Patricia Flynn (eds), *The Politics of Intervention: The United States in Central America*. New York: Monthly Review Press.

Leipziger, Danny M. and Petri, Peter A. 1993. *Korean Industrial Policy, Legacies of the Past and Directions for the Future*. World Bank Discussion Papers, No. 197. Washington DC: The World Bank.

Leipziger, Danny and Vinod Thomas. 1994. 'Roots of East Asia's Success', *Finance and Development*, March: 6–9.

Lele, Uma and Nabi, Ijaz. 1991. *Transitions in Development: the Role of Aid and Commercial Flows*. San Francisco: ICS Press.

Li, K.T. 1988. *The Evolution of Policy Behind Taiwan's Development Success*. New Haven: Yale University Press.

Liang, K.S. and Ching-ing Hou Liang. 1988. 'Development Policy Formation', *Economic Development and Cultural Change*, 36 (3): 571–601.

Lim, Hyun-Chin. 1985. *Dependent Development in Korea 1963–1979*. Seoul: Seoul National University Press.

Lin, C.Y. 1973. *Industrialization in Taiwan. 1946–72*. New York: Praeger.

Lin, Wuu-Long. 1998. 'Strengthening Economic Exchanges Across the Taiwan Strait – Competition and Cooperation', *Industry of Free China*, July: 83–90.

Lucas, Robert Jr. 1990. 'Why Doesn't Capital Flow From Rich to Poor Countries?', *American Economic Review*, 80 (2): 92–6.

MacPhail, Donald and Vaughan, Mary. 1969. 'Comments on Stanford Research Institute Report on Land Reform in Vietnam'. Unpublished document written for the US Agency for International Development.

McCormack, Gavan. 1978. 'Japan and South Korea, 1965–1975', in Gavan McCormack and Mark Selden (eds), *Korea: North and South*. New York: Monthly Review Press.

McCoy, Al. 1971. 'Land Reform as Counter-Revolution', *Bulletin of Concerned Asian Scholars*, 3 (1): 28–9.

Medley, Joseph E. 1989. 'Imperialism and Uneven Development: U.S. Policy in Taiwan and Nicaragua', *Review of Radical Political Economics*, 21 (3): 112–17.

Medley, Joseph E. 1994. 'US Interventions and Economic Development in Small, Poor Countries', *Research in Political Economy*, 14: 221–44.

Meltzer, Allan H. 1998. 'Asian Problems and the IMF', *Cato Journal*, 17 (3).

Mendoza, María Mercedes. 1995. 'First Tentative Agreements', *Barricada International*, 15 (387): 7–9.

Mesa Mora, Vilma. 1989. *La Maquila y La Mujer Trabajadora en Costa Rica*. San José, Costa Rica: Comité Interconfederal Femenino.

Mora, Emilia. 1991. 'Cierre de textileras deja sin empleo a 550', *La Nacion*, 8 August: 5A.

Montgomery, John D. 1967. 'Land Reform and Political Development: Prospects in Vietnam.' Unpublished report written for the US Agency for International Development, Revised Draft, September.

Morrow, Robert B. and Kenneth H. Sherper. 1970. 'Land Reform in South Korea.' Agency for International Development Spring Review Country Paper. Washington DC: USAID.

Morse, Elliot R. and Morse, Victoria A. 1982. *Foreign Aid: An Assessment of New and Traditional Development Strategies*. Boulder, CO: Westview Press.

Myers, Ramon. 1984. 'The Republic of China on Taiwan', *The China Quarterly*, 99: 500–28.

New Directions for the 1970s: Toward a Strategy of Inter-American Development. 1969. (Hearings before the House Subcommittee on Inter-American Affairs). Washington DC: Government Printing Office.

Newsweek. 1991. 'The CIA on the Stump', 21 October: 46–7.

New York Times. 1998. 'As Economies Fail', 2 October: A1/A10.

Ngo, Tak-wing. 1993. 'Civil Society and Political Liberalization in Taiwan', *Bulletin of Concerned Asian Scholars*, 25 (1): 3–15.

Nixon, Richard M. 1973. 'Message from President Nixon to the Congress' Concerning the Foreign Assistance Act of 1973, Department of State Bulletin (28 May 1973).

Numazaki, Ichiro. 1986. 'Networks of Taiwanese Big Business', *Modern China*, 12 (4): 487–534.

Ohmae, Kenichi. 1985. *Triad Power*. New York: The Free Press.

Orellana, José and Morales, José. 1991. 'La AID:-Otro Poder?', *Pensamiento Propio*, 9 (81): 28–36.

Organization for Economic Cooperation and Development (OECD). 1992. *1992 Report*. Paris: OECD.

Ortega, Marvin. 1988. Economist, Managua, Nicaragua, interview with Nan Wiegersma and Nola Reinhardt, 28 July.

Ozawa, Terutomo. 1979. *Multinationalism, Japanese Style*. New Jersey: Princeton University Press.

Page, John. 1994. 'The East Asian Miracle', *Finance and Development*, March: 2–5.

Panarama International. 1991. 'Centoamérica no da la talla', 19 August: 8–9.

Payer, Cheryl. 1974. *The Debt Trap*. New York: Monthly Review Press.

Payer, Cheryl. 1982. *The World Bank*. New York: Monthly Review Press.

Petras, James. 1990. 'Latin America vs. East Asia', *Journal of Contemporary Asia*, 20: 557–9.

Petri, Peter A. 1988. 'Korea's Export Niche: Origins and Prospects', *World Development*, 16 (1): 47–63.

Petri, Peter A. 1995. *Lessons of East Asia*, World Bank Report. Washington DC: The World Bank.

Porter, Gareth. 1975. 'Commodity Import Program.' Unpublished paper written for the Indochina Resources Center, Washington DC.

Powelson, John and Stock, Richard. 1987. *The Peasant Betrayed: Agriculture and Land Reform in the Third World*. Lincoln Institute of Land Policy. Oelgeschlager, Gunn and Hain, Lincoln, Nebraska.

Prosterman, Roy L. 1969. 'Land Reform in Vietnam', *Current History*, 57 (340): 321–32 December.

Prosterman, Roy L. 1970. Speech given at the Spring Review of Land Reform, US Agency for International Development Conference (transcribed by Nan (Hancock) Wiegersma), Washington DC, 2–4 May.

Prowse, Michael. 1993. 'Miracles Beyond the Free Market', *Financial Times of London*, 26 April: 15.

Quandt, Midge. 1991. 'US Aid to Nicaragua: Funding the Right', *Z Magazine*, November: 47–51.

Race, Jeffrey. 1970. 'South Vietnam', *Far Eastern Economic Review*, 20 August.

Ranis, Gustav. 1979. 'Industrial Development', in Galenson (ed.), *Economic Growth and Structural Change in Taiwan*.

Reagan, Ronald. 1984. *'Realism, Strength, Negotiation: Key Foreign Policy Statements of the Reagan Administration'*. Washington, DC: State Department Bureau of Public Affairs: 140–2.

Reed, Edward P. 1979. 'Group Farming in Smallholder Agriculture.' Ph.D. Dissertation. Madison: University of Wisconsin.

Reinhardt, Nola. 1987. 'Agro-exports and the Peasantry in the Agrarian Reforms of El Salvador and Nicaragua', *World Development*, 15 (7): 941–59.

Republic of Korea. 1981. *National Agricultural Cooperative Federation: 1977 Annual Report*. Seoul: NACF.

Republic of Vietnam, National Institute of Statistics. 1968. *Vietnam Statistical Yearbook*. Saigon: National Institute of Statistics.

Rodríguez, Ennio. 1993. *Costa Rica: A Development Path in the 1990s*. Ottawa, Canada: North–South Institute.

Rodrik, Dani. 1994. 'King Kong Meets Godzilla: The World Bank and the East Asian Miracle', Policy Essay No. 11, in Albert Fishlow *et al.* (eds), *Miracle or Design? Lessons from the East Asian Experience*. Washington DC: Overseas Development Council.

Rosa, Herman. 1993. *AID y las Transformaciones Globales en El Salvador*. San Salvador: CRIES.

Rostow, W.W. 1985. *Eisenhower, Kennedy and Foreign Aid*. Austin: University of Texas Press.

Rubin, Robert E. 1998. Testimony before the House Agriculture Committee. Department of the Treasury, Office of Public Affairs internet site, 21 May.

Ruccio, David. 1991. 'When Failure Becomes Success', *World Development*, 19 (10): 1315–34.

Ryrie, William. 1995. *First World, Third World*, New York: St Martin's Press.

Sachs, Jeffrey. 1997. 'IMF is a power unto itself', *Financial Times*, 11 December.

Salazar, José Manuel. 1990. 'El estado y ajuste en el sector industrial', in Claudia Gonzales Vega *et al.* (eds), *Politicas Económicas en Costa Rica, Tomo II*. San José: Academia de Centroamérica.

Saldomando, Angel. 1992. *El Retorno de la AID*. Managua: CRIES.

Sansom, Robert. 1967. *The Economics of Insurgency in the Mekong Delta.* Cambridge: MIT Press.

Scigliano, Robert. 1964. *South Viet Nam: Nation Under Stress.* Boston: Houghton Mifflin.

Seguino, Stephanie. 1994. 'Wages, Income Distribution and Gender in South Korea's Export-Led Economy.' Ph.D. dissertation. Washington: American University.

Shen, T.H. 1964. *Agricultural Development on Taiwan Since World War II.* Ithaca: Cornell University Press.

Shen, T.H. 1970. *The Sino-American Joint Commission on Rural Reconstruction.* Ithaca: Cornell University Press.

Simon, Denis Fred. 1988. 'Technology Transfer and National Autonomy', in Edwin Winckler and Susan Greenhalgh (eds), *Contending Approaches to the Political Economy of Taiwan.*

Simon, Denis Fred. 1992a. 'Taiwan's Strategy for Creating Competitive Advantage', in N.T. Wang (ed.), *Taiwan's Enterprises in Global Perspective.*

Simon, Denis Fred. 1992b. Taiwan's Emerging Technological Trajectory: Creating New Forms of Comparative Advantage', in Denis Fred Simon (ed.), *Taiwan: Beyond the Economic Miracle* Armonk, N.Y.: M.E. Sharpe.

Simon, Lawrence R. and James C. Stephens. 1981. *El Salvador Land Reform, 1980–81: Impact Audit.* Boston: Oxfam America.

Stallings, B. 1986. 'External Finance and the Transition to Socialism in Small Peripheral Societies', in Daniel Fagen *et al.* (eds), *Transition and Development.*

Steele, John T. 1964. 'Compensation for Expropriated Land and Degree of Protection against Inflation.' Land Tenure Center Paper. Madison: University of Wisconsin.

Steinberg, David, Sung-Hwan Ban, W. Donald Bowles and Maureen Lewis. 1984. *Korean Agricultural Services.* Washington DC: USAID.

Stiglitz, Joseph E. 1997. Speech on a Post-Washington Consensus at the United Nations University. Internet Addresshttp://www.wider.unu.edu/ stiglitz.htm. May 1997 version of RFA template.

Stiglitz, Joseph E. 1998a. 'More Instruments and Broader Goals: Moving Toward the Post-Washington Consensus', WIDER Annual Lectures 2. Helsinki: United Nations University World Institute for Development Economics Research.

Stiglitz, Joseph E. 1998b. 'Sound Finance and Sustainable Development in Asia.' Keynote address to the Asia Development Forum. The World Bank Group internet site 12 March.

Stites, Richard. 1982. 'Small-Scale Industry in Yingge, Taiwan', *Modern China,* 8 (2): 247–79.

Stone, Samuel Z. 1989. 'Aspects of Power Distribution in Costa Rica', in Marc Ededman and Joanne Kenen (eds), *The Costa Rican Reader.* New York: Grove Weidenfeld.

Strasma, John. 1988. 'Unfinished Business: Consolidating the Agrarian Reform in El Salvador', in William Thiesenhusen, (ed.), *Search for Agrarian Reform in Latin America.* Boston: Unwin Hyman.

Tchah, Kyun Hi. 1977. *Korean Land Reform and its Effects on Life*. Land Tenure Center. Madison: University of Wisconsin.

Economist, The. 1997. 'New illness, same old medicine.' December 13: 65–6.

Tien, Bui Huu. 1971. Official in Land Reform Directorate, Vietnam, interview with Gareth Porter, 31 August.

Toan, Le Van. 1971. Former Chief of the Land Reform Court, Vietnam, interview with Gareth Porter, 10 November.

Truman, Harry. 1973. 'Truman's Four Point Program', in Henry S. Commager (ed.), *Documents in American History, Volume II*. New Jersey: Prentice Hall.

United Nations. Various years. *1980–1996 International Trade Statistics Yearbooks. Volume I, Trade by Country*. New York: United Nations.

United Nations. 1989. *1989 World Survey on the Role of Women in Development*. New York: United Nations.

United Nations. 1992. *Human Development Report*. New York and Oxford: Oxford University Press.

United Nations. 1994–1998. *Human Development Report(s)*. New York and Oxford: Oxford University Press.

United States Agency for International Development. 1991. *Economic Assistance Strategy for Central America 1991–2000*. Washington DC: Agency for International Development.

United States Department of Commerce. 1975. *Historical Statistics of the United States: Colonial Times to 1970*. Washington DC: United States Government Printing Office.

United States Department of Commerce, Bureau of the Census. 1971–92. *Statistical Abstract of the United States*. Editions 91–112. US Government Printing Office.

United States Department of State. 1997. *1996 Country Reports on Economic Policy and Trade Practices: South Korea*. Washington, DC: Government Printing Office.

United States Department of State Airgram no. A-90. 1971. Subject: Ten Year Update of Village Studies. 2 July.

United States Department of State Telegram. 1970. Subject: Land Reform. No. 6344. 28 April.

United States General Accounting Office. 1992. 'Aid to Nicaragua'. Report to Congressional Requesters. Washington, DC : Government Printing Office.

Vega, Mylena. 1989. 'Autonomous Institutions and the Growth of the Public Sector', in Marc Ededman and Joanne Kenen (eds), *The Costa Rican Reader*. New York: Grove Weidenfeld.

Vanolli, A. Patricia. 1991. Lawyer for cooperatives of women garment workers, Costa Rica, interview with Nan Wiegersma, 10 August.

Wade, Robert. 1984. 'Dirigisme Taiwan-Style', *IDS Bulletin*, 15 (2): 65–70.

Wade, Robert. 1990. *Governing the Market*. Princeton, NJ: Princeton University Press.

Wade, Robert. 1994. 'Is the East Asian Miracle Right?', in Albert Fishlow *et al.*, *Miracle or Design? Lessons from the East Asian Experience*, Policy Essay No. 11.Washington DC: Overseas Development Council.

Wade, Robert and Frank Veneroso. 1998. 'The Asian Crisis: The High Debt Model Vs. The Wall Street–Treasury–IMF Complex'. Russell Sage Foundation (rsage.org) on the Electronic Policy Network.

Waldron, Darryl. 1997. 'Taiwan: An "Omnidimensional" Regional Operations Center?', *The Journal of Developing Areas*, 32 (Fall): 53–70.

Wang, N.T., (ed.) 1992. *Taiwan's Enterprises in Global Perspective*. Armonk, NY: M.E. Sharpe.

Weber, Max. 1980. *The Protestant Ethic and the Spirit of Capitalism* New York: Prentice Hall.

Weisberg, Jacob. 1998. 'Keeping the Boom from Busting', *The New York Times Magazine*, America Online, 19 July: 1–12.

Weiss, Susan. 1991. Interview with employee of the Nicaragua Central Bank, July.

Weisskopf, Thomas E. 1992. 'Toward a Socialism for the Future, in the Wake of the Demise of the Socialism of the Past', *Review of Radical Political Economics*, 24 (3/4): 1–28.

White, Howard. 1992. 'The Macroeconomic Impact of Development Aid: A Critical Survey', *Journal of Development Studies*, 28 (2): 163–240.

White, John. 1974. *The Politics of Foreign Aid*. London: The Bodley Head Ltd.

Wiegersma, Nan. 1988. *Peasant Land, Peasant Revolution*. London and New York: Macmillan Press Ltd. and St Martin's Press.

Wiegersma, Nan. 1994. 'State Policy and the Restructuring of Women's Industries in Nicaragua', in Nahid Aslanbeigui, Steven Pressman and Gale Summerfield (eds), *Women in the Age of Economic Restructuring*. London and New York: Routledge.

Wilkie, Curtis. 1990. 'Blessed is the Peacemaker', *Boston Globe Magazine*, 12 August: 42–3.

Winckler, Edwin and Susan Greenhalgh, (eds.). 1988. *Contending Approaches to the Political Economy of Taiwan*. Armonk, NY: M.E. Sharpe.

Wood, Robert E. 1986. *From Marshall Plan to Debt Crisis*. Berkeley: University of California Press.

World Bank. 1993. *The East Asian Miracle: Economic Growth and Public Policy*. Oxford: Oxford University Press.

World Bank. 1998. *Assessing Aid: What works, What Doesn't and Why*. London: Oxford University Press.

World Development. 1993. 'Islands and Small States: Issues and Policies', Special Issues, 21 (2).

World Development. 1994. 22(4) Special Section: *The World Bank's East Asian Miracle*.

Yamamura, Kozo. 1973. 'General Trading Companies in Japan', in Hugh Patrick (ed.), *Japanese Industrialization and Its Social Consequences*, Berkeley: University of California Press.

Yellen, Janet. 1998. 'Lessons from the Asian Crisis.' Address to the Council on Foreign Relations. President's Council of Economic Advisors internet site, 15 April.

Yoshihara, Kunio. 1981. *Sogo Shosha*. Oxford: Oxford University Press.

Yoshino, M.Y. 1974. 'The Multinational Spread of Japanese Manufacturing Investment Since World War II', *Business History Review*, 48: 357–81.

Yoshino, M.Y. and T. Lifson. 1986. *The Invisible Link*. Cambridge, MA: MIT Press.

Young, Marilyn B. 1991. *The Vietnam Wars: 1945–1990*. New York: Harper Perennial.

Zamora, Sergio. 1991. Director of the Zona Franca in Managua, and the former director of the Cartago Free Trade Zone in Costa Rica in the 1980s, interview with Nan Wiegersma, 29 August and 15 November.

Zimbalist, Andrew. 1988. 'Costa Rica', in Eva Paus (ed.), *Struggle Against Dependence: Nontraditional Export Growth in Central America and the Caribbean*. Boulder and London: Westview Press.

Index